ELOQUENT

A collection of poems encapsulating every day life

Joanne C Hicks

Copyright © 2023 Joanne C Hicks

The right of Joanne C Hicks to be identified as the Author of the Work has been asserted by her in accordance with the Copyright, Designs and Patents Act 1988.

All rights reserved. No part of this publication may be reproduced, distributed, or transmitted in any form or by any means, including photocopying, recording, or other electronic or mechanical methods, without the prior written permission of the publisher, except in the case of brief quotations embodied in critical reviews and certain other non commercial uses permitted by copyright law.

ISBN - 9798851415104

Book cover design by Dave Lewis / Joanne C Hicks

Section images copyright:

Fitness: Margarita *(Pexels)*
Nature: *Pexels*
Man's Best Friend: Julio Cesar Maia *(Pexels)*
General: SevenStorm JUHASZIMRUS *(Pexels)*
People: Dany Paul Eric Binsamou *(Pexels)*
Seasons: Nguyen Tran *(Pexels)*
Covid-19: Anna Tarazevich *(Pexels)*
Queen: *wallpapercave*

Dedication

I would like to dedicate this book to my family who have always been very supportive, encouraging and positive about my poetry and writing. Thank you for always believing in me.

I also would like to give my thanks to Dr Chintha Dissanayake who helped me find the right path and gave me the strength to change my life. The quote below sums it up. I do not know who to credit this quote to but it popped up on my Facebook feed at a time when I was wrangling about which way to go and what to do next.

"When you stop chasing the wrong things, you give the right things a chance to catch you."

Remember to never stop dreaming, learning and growing.

Contents

Fitness & Health
Eat The Rainbow - Begin To Glow	3
In Cahoots With Fitness...	4
Diets - The Struggle Is Real	6
On Borrowed Time …… Eat It!	8
Sunny Summer Hazy Days - You May Need To Avert Your Gaze...	9
That Handy Extra Shelf…	10
Drive By Diet...	12

Nature In All Its Glory And Beauty
Environmental Revolution	15
A Day On The Beach	16
A Force Of Nature	18
Life Is Like A Beautiful Flower	20
I Am But Just A Bumble Bee!	22
Captivating Caldey Island	25
Majestic Trees Standing Tall	26

Man's Best Friend
Man's Best Friend	29
A Doggy Welcome!	30
Ode To Benji Boo	32
A Dog Should Be For Life	34
Tree Hugging Beast	36
The Lion King – Played By Benji	38
An Untimely End!	39
Benji And Lucy Lou Are Off On A Trip	40
Who Broke The Dog?	42
The Rainbow Bridge	44
Pink Fluffy Slippers - Set Free	46
Ode To Stalker Steve (The Baby Seagull)	47
Pesky Pigeons Playing Games…	48
The Big Fat Seagull... King Of Tenby	50
The Pigeon's Demise	51

Faith & Reflections
The Here And Now	55
Brexit Shaken Not Stirred!	56
VE Day 2020 - 75 Years On...	58
A Glimmer Of Hope And Light	60
The Bright Red Door	62
Wasting Away	64
How Far Is It Between Earth And Heaven?	66
We Live In A Beautiful World	68
A Hole In Your Soul	69
Letters To Heaven	70
Who Is Your Shepherd?	71
Faith - A Journey Of Trust	72
The Messenger From Heaven	74
I Hope There Is A Heaven…	76
Black Dog	77
One Grain Of Sand	78
The Earth Has Quaked	79
The Town That Is No More…	80

People - Family, Friends And Life!
Dad	83
Hide And Seek	84
The River Of Life	86
In A World Where You Can Be Anything	87
The Glass Of Life	88
She Danced	89
Your Invisible Cape	90
You've Got This	92
Reclaim Your Youth - Be Brave!	93
The Scars Of Life	94
What Is Ordinary?	95
Child's Play	96
Battle Lines Are Drawn	98
That Old Jumper	99
Wet Pants	100

It's Friday! It's Friday!	103
Wrinkly, Crinkly Skin…	104
Life - The Tapestry We Weave	106
Me Time - Never Feel Guilty About It!	108
Tomorrow Without You	109
You Chose To Cross The Final Bridge	110
That Song	112
Reflections Of You…	113
Touch It - Feel It - No Live It	116
Riches Of Life	118
Are You There?	120
Open Your Soul	121
Sands Of Time	122
The Deep Grip Of Grief	124
Shine Like A Star	126
A Glass Of Wine Is Just Fine!	127
Loneliness	128
A Broken Mind	130
My Sexy Beau…	132
Words	133
A Snapshot In Time…	

Seasons

Weightless Delicate Delight	137
Spring - A Lifetime Away…	138
Autumn's Leafy Gifts To Mother Nature	140
Nature's Winter Wonderland	142
The Great British Weather	144
Food For Festive Thought	145
A Truly Special Day	146
The Best Things In Life Are Free	148
Spring Has Sprung…	149

Covid-19

In The Stillness We Will Find Hope	153
The Year That Changed The World	154
You Say Hello…	156
A Faceless Future?	158
Behind The Mask	160
Lord You Were With Us	162
Lunch Anyone?	164
Distant Memories…	166
I Long To…	168
Covid-19 Silver Lining…	169
Natures Playground	170
Hands Face Space...	172
Home Schooling - Oh What Fun!	173
Rainbow Nails…	176
NHS Heroes	177
The Real Heroes 2020	178
Summer Vibes - Coz There's No Christmas Tribes!	180
What's Your Value?	181

Our Queen

Lilibet 1926-2022	185
Monarch, Leader, Woman And Mother	186
Our Queen 1926-2022	188
A Corgi's Love	190
Your Final Journey 1926-2022	192

About The Author

Fitness & Health

Eat The Rainbow - Begin To Glow

I rest my arms upon my belly
It's wobbling like a beautiful jelly.
I don't really mind my muffin top fat
So long as I'm healthy I am happy with that.

However my diet has been pretty shocking
Those cakes and biscuits I've been a rocking.
I need to stop and take stock of it all
At least I will bounce should I have a great fall.

Tomorrow I will start, I promise I will
I will stop stuffing food down - just eat my fill.
The world is full of a rainbow of food
So why eat the junk when you are feeling blue?

It seems I like puddings, chocolates and sweets
I'm also obsessed with my daily portion of meat.
So I'm sitting here talking myself fit
Of my rolls, lumps and bumps I must get a grip!

So as the sun rises tomorrow - or maybe the rain just stops
I shall stop eating everything until my belly goes pop!
A rainbow of food I shall endeavour to eat
If I could go to the gym that would also be neat.

So wish me luck folks, as my willpower is low
I may end up face planting a whole chocolate gateau!
I will find my resolve and leave the junk well alone
Although when I see it my heart will just groan.

That junk food is addictive - my terrible vice
It all just tastes so terribly yummy and nice!
But I will think of my rainbow if I'm feeling weak
And try to remember junk sticks to your butt cheeks!

In Cahoots With Fitness...

"Are we going - are we going - you know you said you would?
You said you were going - you know you really should."
Say the voices in my head knowing I'd like to go to bed.
I really could stay at home and watch TV instead.

Reluctantly I consider the proposition that's been made.
You remind yourself you are, after all, on a personal crusade.
I find my insides screeching - staying in would be just peachy
But those voices in your head are really rather screechy.

I drag my weary body off the oh-so-comfy sofa.
I'm going to go and swim like a forceful supernova!
I pack my little rucksack and sling it on my back.
I expect by the time it's Christmas I'll be nurturing a six-pack.

I've had a very busy day running here and there.
I've smiled oh so sweetly and been rather debonair.
Up and down the stairs, my bum hardly on my chair.
The thought of going swimming is just too much to bear.

I'm finally on my way and I'm feeling rather proud
I finally conceded and to that pesky voice I bowed!
Pah I put that voice to sleep and now I cannot hear a peep
From the sofa to the pool truly was a giant leap.

Besides if the truth were known there's more than meets the eye
I need to go swimming - I did eat that mouth-watering mince pie
My stinky hair needs washing and I'm not even joshing.
It's dark and cold outside so maybe this beats jogging.

I soon feel the water washing all around my limbs.
I'm sure when I get out of the pool I will be super slim!
The troubles of the day begin to slip away.
I will be ready for Red January come what may.

So 40 minutes later and lots of lengths completed.
Those stress demons in my mind have truly been defeated.
My head is crystal clear and I'm feeling quite refreshed.
Who knew a dip in water would leave me at my best.

So when you've had a busy day and you're feeling very tired.
You know if you go do something it will leave you feeling wired.
Dig deep my friends – right down into your boots.
Who knows you and fitness may end up in cahoots!

Diets - The Struggle Is Real

I've gone all day without a treat
Not even a single sneaky sweet.
Well ok there was an incident in the kitchen
Which involved the pesky bread bin.
But I've tried so hard to be strong
Why are treat-less days so long?

I fear that Shrove Tuesday is looming
So many pancakes I will be consuming.
I best sign up for a treat-less Lent
40 days of discontent.
Chocolate bars luring me in
Knowing they are my deadly sin.

Why oh why is food so nice
It's my poor thighs that pay the price.
Everywhere seems to be
Naughty things for you - for me.
I've gone all morning and not eaten
I think this diet has me beaten.

I slowly climb upon the bathroom scales
Which seem to shout out, "Ahoy beached whale."
I look down in despair
Another pound on they declare!
That can't be right, it can't be true
Now I'm feeling truly blue!

I mean I've been so very healthy
I should be feeling mighty wealthy.
I mean the struggle I've endeavoured
My stomach thinks my throat's been severed.
How long - how long has it been?
Feels like ages I've been eating clean.

I check the calendar with such hope
Oh flip I feel like such a dope.
I count the days that can't be right
I felt time was going like the speed of light.
Has it really only been a week?
No wonder I've got the same physique.

Diets - the struggle is real - but that said beauty comes from within. So don't let the mirror, scales or people rule your life - just be you. Happy, healthy and wise!

On Borrowed Time - Eat It!

A bar of chocolate in the drawer,
Is always sitting on borrowed time.
It's like you can almost hear it roar,
Eat me - go on - it won't be a crime.

You sit and ignore that nagging voice,
That seems to get louder as the night goes on.
You think of your diet - yes make the right choice.
You will have dropped a dress size before long.

I mean you've been on this diet for a whole 6 hours
So your body is already feeling wonderfully fit.
What if you ran up and down all the stairs?
That would counter balance the calories wouldn't it?

I mean everyone deserves a treat every now and then
You have eaten like a church mouse most of the day.
You could always just start the whole diet thing again?
I mean let's be honest it's a week until you weigh.

Oh yes that poor bar of chocolate is on borrowed time
It's sitting nice and cosy and probably feeling quite lonely.
Nestled in the drawer, which is not too far from the wine.
Why don't they make the nice things calorie free - if only!

I will just eat the chocolate and start over tomorrow
I'm sure I've probably lost a pound or two today.
Oh maybe I should have some juicy, red tomatoes
Blow it - I'll get the forbidden fruit and munch away.

Eat the chocolate
Light the posh candles
Use the bath bombs
Drink the wine
Enjoy yourself
Everything in moderation!

Sunny Summer Hazy Days - You May Need To Avert Your Gaze...

I never thought the day would come
I'd put on shorts to go for a run.
But my car was telling me it was 28 degrees
Wow that heat could bring me to my knees!

So on went the shorts - out came the thighs
Maybe I should not have eaten all those pies.
I won't be put off - I won't be ashamed
My fitness needs to be reclaimed!

So I will go out proudly - legs on display
Keep on going - come what may
For we all come in lots of shapes and sizes
And for perseverance - your fitness rises!

That Handy Extra Shelf…

Isn't it handy, don't you think?

Your body develops an extra shelf.

I'm talking of course about my rounded tummy.

It's here I can let my hands just rest.

It's also quite handy for balancing chocolate bars.

And it's a brilliant help when eating my dinner,

As I find it keeps my plate of goodies stable.

I feel a little dismayed when I look in the mirror.

That visual reminder of why people say "muffin top".

A finely formed rim around my waist.

Distinctively tyre shaped but soft and squidgy.

I look back at old photos when I thought I was fat.

Seems quite ludicrous now my body's rounded out.

So here I am - another new year.

No New Years resolutions for me - I can't keep them.

But a commitment to try and improve my diet!

So wish me luck as I try to be good.

Mmm maybe I need to stop baking biscuits and cakes!

Do you know what though at the end of the day

Your size doesn't matter - it's your mind and your health!

Money can buy the most wonderful things.

But no amount of money can buy you good health!

So let's all be more accepting of our bodies.

Focus on good health and just being kind!

Drive By Diet...

By the time I've covered 10 miles I feel I've already lost a stone
I mean I'm mentally convinced I am already just skin and bones,
I breathe in deep to suck everything in - yes I definitely think I'm thinner
I start to think that maybe I will just have a small pudding after my dinner.

Then it's that moment as you drive along and pass those runners in a throng
Oh yes I will definitely take up running again, I'm sure they'd let me tag along?
So by the time you've gone another mile, you are now running marathons
Mentally you are hanging up more running medals - gold, silver and bronze.

So by the time you pull up at your destination you've slimmed and toned your tired body
In your mind you've changed your life - your body no longer worn and shoddy!
You leap out of your car with a determined stride and skip in through the front door
You flop on to the sofa, your mind already straying - not so sure now about your food war!

Slowly your mind is saying, you could just start tomorrow - I mean this day is almost done
Besides you've got that chocolate bar half eaten and... salad - well you've none!
Yes we will start again tomorrow, I will get myself organised it's going to be a breeze
Well you do first need to polish off the crisps, biscuits, cakes and cheese.

Nature, In All Its Glory And Beauty

Environmental Revolution

I wonder if God is sat looking down from upstairs
At this world he created and for which he deeply cares.

I wonder if he's sat there with his head in his hands
Looking at the destruction humans have brought upon the land.

I wonder if he looked on in complete despair
As humans have acted like we just don't care.

I wonder if he knew that our plans would destroy our planet?
Only now we realise that the environment isn't like granite!

Weather so destructive as it beats it's daily path
Beating suns and pouring rain releasing its full wrath.

Humans are shouting let's use our natural resources
We have to stop the onslaught from these nature forces.

Let's stop the use of plastic, which is now choking our deep seas
Stop consuming processed junk, which is causing disease.

Stop fuelling all our lives from a bank of fossil fuels
Let's use the sun, wind and sea instead - they are our natural tools.

I wonder if God sits and looks and thinks they'll work it out
I wonder now if the facts are beginning to erode doubt?

I wonder if God is sad that humans can be such a destructive race
As we beat a path to move "forward" at a never ending pace.

I wonder if God sits and knows his faith in us will win
As we start to clean our act up - let the green revolution begin.

A Day On The Beach

Birds flying up, oh so high
Way up into the marshmallow like sky.

Kites dancing around, up and down
Like sheets billowing all around.

Birds swooping over us ready to dive
Like they are coming in for a high five.

Dogs with their owners; allowed to run free
Tails wagging, barking - so full of glee.

Birds flying lower - harmless creatures or so it seems
Until they swoop in to steal your ice-cream!

Little children paddling in the sea
Giggling and laughing - oh so free.

Couples walking hand in hand
Their bodies boasting a glowing tan.

An elderly couple watching the sunset
Neither wants to leave just yet.

Teenagers playing a game of football
Soon it becomes a free for all.

So much laughter, tears, fun and joy
For every man, woman, girl and boy.

Then the light begins to fade
Just one couple on the promenade.

Then they have all gone home
The birds are now all alone.

All you can hear is the sound of the sea
Waves crashing on the sand so subtly.

The day is over, the day is done
24 hours since it begun...

A Force Of Nature

The sea swirling, swishing, sloshing around and around.
The waves crashing onto rocks, a somewhat soothing sound.

The sea that provides such healing qualities,
A place of family fun and endless frivolities.

A place to sit in quiet contemplation
Helps us sit and discover our core foundations.

A myriad of colours, rich green and deep blue
That invites you to dip your toes into.

A force, which changes the world around us,
Environmental changes which we should discuss.

Waves crashing down upon the shore,
Giving up its secrets and so much more.

Shells, stones and sea glass scattered upon the shoreline
Collected by children, laughing, in the summer sunshine.

A landscape, which changes hour by hour,
We sit in awe and wonder at its superpower.

A force that brings pleasure but also such pain,
As those who lost their lives struggled in vain.

A force to be treated with so much respect.
A force being disrupted by the greenhouse effect.

We still have so much to learn and we all have so much to do.
Seas suffocated and polluted by plastic shouldn't remain a subject taboo.

A vast array of creatures and plants live in the oceans and seas,
We stand and observe them as we feel that cool sea breeze.

This mighty expanse pulled by the gravitation of the moon
Influencing tides - two forces of nature in perfect attune.

So just take a moment and stop, sit and listen
As the sun dances on the water and everything glistens.

So take a moment to say a prayer for those lost in the oceans
Spend a moment with nature and connect deeply with your emotions.

Life Is Like A Beautiful Flower

Do you not think that life is like a flower?
That rises up seemingly as a tall as a tower.
It starts off in the dark like a baby in the womb
Then bam - it emerges from its earthy tomb.
All small and weak at first, needing food and nurture
It stretches up and up until it really can't go any further.

Then it starts to open up, no longer shy and retiring
Bees, birds, insects and humans all stopping and admiring.
For now the flowers showing off it's glorious blooms
A burst of petals like a bird showing off its plumes.
Loved and nurtured it's got so much to share
The smell of its perfume is everywhere.

And then its beauty starts to fade
Its petals colours gradually lose their shade.
Then the petals start to slowly drop
Some faster than others, some just flop.
Some fade away faster as they cannot weather the storm
Some have the strength to dance through the rainfall.

The final petals slowly fall drifting on the breeze
This wonderful plant no longer able to feed the bees.
It's helped so many in its life and now its time is done
It's probably seen sadness, tears, laughter, happiness and fun.
If it could think it may feel it's touched and helped no-one
But this would not be true for we all know what it's done.

So don't ever sit and wonder how your own life touches others
It will be the little things you've done - maybe even undercover!
We grow in some way with every day that passes
You don't have to try and reach out to the masses.
Just be yourself and kind and caring
Giving a little and maybe sharing.
Like the flowers we all come in different guises
We really do come in many, many sizes!

So it's fine to be different - stand proud and tall
Never shy away feeling insignificant and small.
You really will be someone's rock
You may well be their ticking clock.
We all are beautiful in our own way
So stay strong come what may.
Push out your petals for all to see
Sing and dance and jump with glee.

If you look and think others are better than you
Don't be silly, don't be a fool.
Find your inner strength and believe in you
We all have something to offer - it's true!
You may not know it when you are in the storm
Hang on to your petals, don't let them be torn.
Your truly awesome so remember to believe in you
For when you're gone you will want them to know you truly flew.

I Am But Just A Bumble Bee!

I lead a very busy life, buzzing here and buzzing there,
You will notice me immediately as I sport rather funky hair!
It is a stunning black and yellow; I wear it as a striking stripe
But my coat, it comes with lots of stereotypes.

You people think because I buzz I must be rather angry
I think that actually I am really rather spangly!
But still you hear me buzzing by
And all your arms - up do fly.

That buzzing sound that I omit
Is merely my wings on the beat.
I move them oh so very fast
The wind creates a mighty blast.

It seems you hear me from afar
You take that stance - ready to spar.
But please don't hurt me - can't you see
I am just a harmless bumblebee.

I have a purpose don't you know.
I land on flowers and make the pollen blow.
My wings create that magic beat
Nectar is my desired treat.

I love to land amongst the flowers
Sometimes I have to dodge the pesky showers.
I love it when the sun shines through
I can collect my nectar - my home brew.

I am a very busy bee - flying around from flower to flower
Lavender, roses, and marigolds - I bob around with a superpower.
I only have a tiny window - not much time to collect my gold.
Then I see you, over there, what is that thing that you hold?

Oh no, here we go - please don't let that sight be true!
That familiar dance we have to do.
There you stand with your menacing frown
A rolled up paper - ready to bring me down.

I fly away as fast as I can
But you are swiping, like an evil man!
Oh stop it, stop it - please don't hurt me
I am just a harmless fat bumblebee.

My wings transparent - my fuzzy body that is rotund
With one swipe I would be stunned.
Leave me alone with your giant fly swatter
Your eyes just focussed on my slaughter.

My heart is beating oh so hard
I must not inadvertently drop my guard.
I could just use my secret weapon
My sting, which is as tough as Teflon.

I really don't want to sting you
I want to just say adieu!
Your flailing arms are really swinging
Is that the Daily Mail you're flinging?

At last it seems you are giving up
Does that make you the runner up?
That little girl is pulling hard upon on your arm
"Stop," she's saying - "the bees, you cannot cause them harm."

What is this that she is saying?
A reprieve for me from a slaying?
"Daddy stop," she pleads again
"Please let me just explain."

"We need the bees in our lives
Let them go back to their hives.
They pollinate the flowers and plants
Besides Dad - you are in your underpants!"

"Come inside and leave him be
Let him go - let him flee."
I hover a little and watch them go.
Inside I feel a little glow.

I am free once more to do my work
I allow myself a little smirk.
I land upon a beautiful petal
Here I sit and finally settle.

The sun is beating on my wings
I listen to the birds as they sing.
I must get on - I must get back
The Queen will think I have begun to slack!

So when you see a busy bee
Remember that it is them we need.
They are so important in our lives
So let's all make sure they truly thrive!

Captivating Caldey Island

Waves gently landing on your golden sands
Wave after wave washing onto this holy land
Flowers bursting out in a kaleidoscope of colours
Blooming over and over for so many summers

Birds swoop and sway in the deep blue skies
A feast for our soul before our eyes
I step on the sand and it seeps through my toes
An enchanting island that time simply froze

The sun on the sea glistening like angels kisses
Through the woodland peeps out all of nature's riches
Bees, butterflies, birds hiding in the beautiful bountiful bushes
In this perfect piece of paradise no one thing rushes

Churches tucked away amongst the majestic trees
Tranquil and perfect - where your soul can be free
So many secrets shared between you and your maker
Simple headstones for those gone to a place even greater

A slice of paradise surrounded by serene seas
Is this what heaven is like - is this a gentle tease?
I lie down and sink into the soft, smooth, silky sand
I'm sure that I feel the whole of nature holding my hand.

Majestic Trees Standing Tall

You stand majestically surveying your land
Alongside a river which around you it wends
You sit small and lost in the foothills of mountains
Dwarfed by their greatness but you still stand divine

Your long reaching branches provide shelter to many
At the top sits a dark raven and to him it's his castle
Your branches provide the vital cover he needs
Camouflage comes from your fresh green leaves

Branches like blankets wrap and hide all life underneath
A sanctuary and home, which creatures can live beneath
So much you see standing tall on the landscape
How many times have you've been an escape

Secrets whispered underneath your strong trunk
Secrets, which you and your branches will keep
Standing like a tower for year after year
My, if only we knew all that you've heard.

Man's Best Friend

Man's Best Friend

I look at you
You look at me
Neither of us makes a sound
But we both can see

You tilt your head
And I tilt mine
I smile and laugh
You stay transfixed

No words exchanged
Just meaningful looks
I'm sure you understand me
You know that I love you

I shake my head and walk away
You stand up and follow me
I stop and look into your eyes
Faithful, loyal and dependable

My best friend
We've never even spoken
But you have my heart
Unconditional love right there

Dogs - man's best friend.

A Doggy Welcome!

When you have a dog there is one thing that you learn
When you leave the house, for that money you must earn
There will always be a welcome home
From your dogs - who you had left, all alone.

They'll bound towards you in full flight
Jumping up with all their might.
She's back, she's back - their yelps will say
They'll try and lick you come what may.

Their tails will wag like planes propellers
Their jumping skills are really quite stellar!
They'll twist and turn to reach your face
Whatever you were holding is now displaced!

Their joy is clear for all to see
Wagging tails and yelps of glee.
The thing that really makes you smile
Is you've only been gone a wee short while!

Unconditional love I think they call it
We pick up their poop - we can't ignore it!
They damage our brand new dining room chairs
When I'm lying resting they will come and pull my hair.

They sit with their head on our laps as we eat
Hoping we will throw them a tasty treat.
You look at those eyes, all forlorn
Oh go on - you can share my popcorn.

They lie on our laps as we watch the T.V.
Only moving when they need a wee.
They follow you round from room to room
That even extends into the bathroom.

And when you stand and shout out "treats"
They return faster than Olympic athletes.
They'll sit, lie down and offer their paw
All for that juicy bone they want to gnaw.

I love my dogs - they bring me cheer
Despite the fact they chew my ears!
They truly are man's best friend
And may this relationship never end.

Ode To Benji Boo

Sometimes I think I'm the only one who loves you Benji Boo
You are definitely my Tigger to my portly Winnie the Pooh.
You are so full of energy bouncing all around
It's true; your paws are barely on the ground.

There are some moments when you are also like Houdini
Popping through the conifer hedge - almost routinely.
One look back then off you trot a million miles an hour
Following that cat scent because to you it smells of flowers.

I swear I see you smirking as I'm bringing up the rear
You take another look at me and move it up a gear.
Eventually the game is over and home again we go
It's getting very tiresome I will have you know!

Sometimes it is known for even Tiggers to take a rest
And when you snuggle up to me it really is the best.
I love the way you look at me with your gorgeous deep brown
    eyes
Then you'll leap up pulling at my hair taking me quite by surprise.

You must think you are popular as we all call out your name.
But really it's because we don't enjoy your little game.
You love to steal our tissues and eat them if you can
We've had to introduce a complete wastepaper bin ban.

But we wouldn't be without you, truly we would not
Well maybe Georgie boy doesn't like you a lot.
He thinks you smell quite badly and he hates your Tigger ways.
But I think you really melt his heart with your supersonic gaze.

So if you see me and my boy out running around the place,
I give you word of warning this Tigger needs his space.
See that monkey Benji Boo will want to come and play
So he starts to jump and bark and you may think you are his prey!

He really doesn't mean it he's quite a sociable dog
He just can't stand the lead and the fact he has to jog!
So yes I love my Tigger with all his faults and flaws
From his floppy ears, wagging tail - I even smell his paws.

A Dog Should Be For Life

Another long, dark lonely night
Sat pondering my awful plight.
I sit and watch the sun rise up
A sight I loved when I was a pup.

I bury my head into my bed
At least here I do get fed.
That lovely lady takes me walkies
I cock my head while she tells me stories.

I look deep into her dark brown eyes
Maybe she needs me to apologise.
I'm not sure why - I've done no wrong
But she won't take me home where I belong.

She comes each day to take me out
But leaves me here no matter how loud I shout.
I don't understand what it is I've done
I think back to the days when life was fun.

I had a family who loved me dearly
I must have done something wrong, clearly.
One day they bundled me into the car
We took a journey that was so bizarre.

I tried to comfort them on the way
As tears streamed down their faces.
Then they left me at this strange place
They said I'd be kept warm and safe.

And here I've been for oh so long
I no longer have a home where I belong.
People come and sit and cuddle me
But none of them set me free.

So here I sit in this caged, suffocating prison
Sitting, waiting to be a family's new addition.
I long to lie in a sun filled garden again
With a trip to the beach every now and then.

I curl up and listen to my roommates
What if I'm stuck here in this place?
I had a family - I had a home.
And now I sit here - all alone.

Tree Hugging Beast

Most dog owners have normal dogs
They don't need to appear in random blogs.
They trot along tails up high
Noses pointing to the sky.

My little fur baby seems a bit crazy
He's definitely far from lazy.
He loves to go on muddy walks
All the way it's like he talks.

Singing here and whining there
People passing don't half stare
A singing pooch is quite a feat
It's truly something hard to beat.

But singing isn't where it ends
Although that drives you round the bend.
He has this rather strange obsession
Which does help get out any aggression.

You see he has a real dear friend
It's something that tends to bow and bend.
Most dogs love to chase a stick
Run after a ball that you kick.

But not my Benji oh no no no
He finds a branch hanging down low.
Jumps aboard and doesn't let go
How he does it - we don't know.

He hangs on tight with all his might
Swings about because he's so light.
He's hanging on bouncing up and down
Lucy Lou rolling in fox poop she's found.

But he doesn't stop there, oh no not him
Swinging on branches is just one of his things.
He's a modern day boy don't you know
Tree hugging is also in his portfolio.

He surveys his land as he walks
Maybe looking for a tree that talks.
Once he's found his chosen tower
Up he climbs with amazing power.

Perhaps he's hunting squirrels or chasing birds
There he goes singing his doggy words.
He stands so proud up his tree
Saying to all look at me.

He's got no fear of any height
I'm sure he's going to take flight.
He stands there oh so proud and tall
Despite the fact he's only small.

So when we are out for a stroll
Please remember Benji has no self-control.
He thinks he's a bird or a plane
Or maybe he just needs a lion's mane.

Good job he's got Sally keeping him safe
She really is his best human mate.
Dog walker extraordinaire
His doggy adventures she loves to share.

The Lion King – Played By Benji

My dog climbs trees don't you know
I think he does it just for show.
Maybe he thinks he is a monkey
Or perhaps he was feeling a little spunky.

Maybe he thought he was in the Lion King
I swear I thought he was about to sing.
The Circle of Life or Hakuna Matata
Why it could have been quite a sonata!

Oh please don't fall from that tree
Or find a nest full of bumblebees!
He really does not seem to care
As for me - I'm now turning to prayer!

He seems to want to go up higher
Next he will want a high wire.
Oh good - relief - he's coming back down
Thank goodness all four paws are back on the ground.

I swear though when he got back down
He grinned and turned back around.
I swear I heard him begin to sing
"Oh I just can't wait to be King!"

An Untimely End!

If you find me on the road
Know there's been a terrible episode.
If I'm laid out like a starfish
No longer like a whirling dervish.

Then I'd say the dog is to blame.
For this is what I do proclaim.
I have a dog called Lucy Lou,
Who gives no warning when she's does a poo.

Out it comes while she walks on,
She just stops once she's done.
So down I go, bag in hand
To pick up her poop strand.

Problem is - it's in the road
And that's how my story will be told.
Ah yes, we found her pancaked on the road.
It was the ending that she did forebode!

Benji And Lucy Lou Are Off On A Trip

She's taking us in the car
I wonder if we are going far?
I am so excited I can't keep quiet
Come on, let's start a riot!

She's put us in the back together.
Oh I do hope this is a trip for pleasure.
Let's sing a song, loud and sharp
Intertwined with a few loud barks.

I think we may be heading to the beach.
Let's use this time to plan our siege.
There's bound to be other dogs there.
Man, maybe there will be dogs everywhere!

I'm buzzing, I can't stop whining.
Hey, we can even go off rock climbing.
We can dip our paws into the rock pools.
Do zoomies like a couple of fools.

Oh hang on a minute - what's this?
She's turned off and telling us to sit.
This road does look a bit familiar.
Something is a foot - this is peculiar.

Oh no I really don't like this.
I'm changing my whining to a higher pitch.
She's taking us to that horrible place.
I'm desperately doing a memory retrace.

Yes it is the place - the place that I hate.
Oh man I hope this visit is for you mate.
Last time I was here he stuck his finger up my bottom.
He also rather rudely said my breath was rotten!

I'm sitting in the back, simpering and shaking.
Well to be honest I'm actually quaking.
Here she comes to get me out
Ready Lucy Lou - do your pout.

I dig my heels in and put my head down.
I will do my best to give her the run around.
It's no good she's dragged me in.
I'm sitting here completely on pins.

The man comes out and looks around.
Well this is it - the final countdown.
What delights will it be today?
Prodded and poked much to my dismay.

The man steps forward and I cower down.
I need to escape so I look all around.
The man shouts out "Lucy Lou".
Ha ha - I turn - that's you! That's you!

Your face has dropped, your ears are down.
But me whoop whoop I'm dancing round.
The man turns to walk away
He stops and has one more thing to say…

Bring Benji through as well…
What me? I don't even feel unwell!
It's no good resisting she's dragging me through.
Oh heck - I think I may need the loo!

Who Broke The Dog?

I think my dog is broken
I know you think that's mad
It's something that can't go unspoken
He really is shockingly bad.

He's got a glorious warm home
With blankets, love and food
Sometimes with a juicy bone
But his behaviour is just rude!

If we are walking down the road
And he spies you from afar
That's it, he's off in barking mode
He's lost yet another doggy star.

When you come to visit us
It's really not much better
All he wants is lots of fuss
I should restrain him in some fetters

When a letter drops upon the mat
It has to be fully vetted
He's on it in a flash just like that
The letter sadly lies beheaded.

He loves to chase a stick
At this he's really good
Trouble is he really can be thick
Climbing trees like the king of the wood

I swear that boy thinks he's a squirrel
As he scurries up those trees.
My heart is in my mouth as he's surely in peril
I'm just left begging - come down - please!

We take him down to the beach
For a glorious run about
An old dog, new tricks, you cannot teach
In the sand he buries his furry snout.

But once the day is over
His antics done and dusted
It's the sofa that he decides to takeover
He almost looks like he could be trusted

He curls up in a ball, snug on your lap
A picture of tranquillity
You've been lured into his trap
He no longer looks like a barking liability

But even though he's broken
You love him warts and all
When he's gone you'll be heartbroken
He truly is my be and end all.

The Rainbow Bridge

It's only a dog you will hear people say
But they've not been there for every birthday.
They weren't there when you fell knee deep in the mud.
Or when you ate all my plants as they were coming into bud.

They weren't there when you ate the cheese you shouldn't have.
Or all the times I had pleaded with you to just please behave.
When you bounded in the sea like you were some sort of mermaid.
You would jump over those waves - never really afraid.

They weren't there when you lay down by my side.
When I felt really poorly and I couldn't open my eyes.
They weren't there for all of our thousands of walks.
When you'd roll in something that had been left by a fox.

They weren't there when you would lie loyally at my feet.
Or when you escaped and I chased you down our street.
They weren't there when I was feeling sad, lonely and forlorn.
And you sat and licked my tears from my hand where they'd fallen.

Then I start to notice that you've slowed down a bit.
Maybe now you are no longer quite as fit.
You still love your walks but we don't go so far.
You seem to prefer longer rides out in the car.

Your coat not quite so shiny and your eyes not so bright.
I tell myself your endless unconditional love I will requite.
Then I wake up one morning and see you are gone.
Your life slipped away at the break of the dawn.

My heart floods with sadness and tears fill my eyes.
I fall down beside you and weep and just cry.
The pain that I feel is unbearably hard.
And I know that my heart will be forever scarred.

So goodbye my loyal friend until we meet again.
And I hope over time I will feel a lot less pain.
You were my best friend and I will miss you each day.
The doggy rainbow bridge is beckoning you to come and stay.

To all my doggy friends who know the pain of saying goodbye to your four-legged friend when they make their final journey over the rainbow bridge.

Pink Fluffy Slippers - Set Free

I had some new slippers, all fluffy and pink.
I walked in the bedroom and I felt my heart sink.
My beautiful slippers lay all tattered and torn.
My pink furry babies I stood there, my slippers to mourn.

I look all around me but you are nowhere to be found.
Come on, where are you, you sweet pesky hound!
I spent a small fortune on an array of dog toys.
Some even making that high pitched squeaking noise!

My poor beautiful slippers, worn only once.
I look down at this fluff fest, just wanting to wince.
I know you are here, just hiding away.
I will come and find you, come what may.

I gently call out your name as I've a new game to play.
I have lovely doggy treats and I'm giving them away!
Come out, come out, wherever you are.
Come on my fur baby - you can't have gone far!

Then I look down and see it, your give away sign.
Under the bed, there's a wagging tail and a small whine.
Aha I have got you - you can't get away!
I am your master - the one you obey!

I call out your name, so sickly and sweet.
There is nowhere that you can beat a retreat.
You crawl out on your belly and lift up your eyes.
You, you made sure my slippers met their demise!

I look down at you, as you crawl out on your belly.
Your bottom jaw wobbling like a big bowl of jelly.
You lift up your paw and cock your head to the side.
This one simple action - I look deep into your eyes.

Guess I don't need my slippers - well, not at this time
I mean chewing my slippers is hardly a war crime.
I lay my hand on your head and you gaze up at me.
Ok boy, I guess you thought you just set my slippers free.

Ode To Stalker Steve (The Baby Seagull)

I've got a new friend - we've become quite close
He just suddenly appears from out of the shadows.
I've nicknamed him Steve because he can't talk
In fact, if I'm honest - all he can do is squawk.

You see Steve is a seagull but just a baby boy
He's really docile and I think a little coy.
He's sits and waits for me outside the shop.
He struts about and his head does a wee bob.

But despite all his looks of love and care
I'm feeling a great sense of despair
For while Steve looks quite cute and sweet
Deep down he's a rascal preying on fresh meat.

Before too long Steve will be a master thief
Your encounter with your pasty may be brief!
Once he's all grown he will steal your food
Sadly he will be one quite cunning dude.

So whilst I stop and give him a little smile
I know this friendship can only last a short while.
For before very long I will be chasing him away
So that your food on its plate will stay.

Pesky Pigeons Playing Games...

A game of cat and mouse is in play

It's been going on pretty much every day.

You see there is a very special customer at the coffee shop.

He doesn't walk, he sort of waddles, well more like a hop.

He's very brave, bold and brash

This customer doesn't carry card or cash.

But still every day he tries to get to the best table

Sometimes he bring his wife, I've nicknamed her Mabel.

His head jerking back and forth as he waddles through the door.

As soon as he's inside my feet don't hit the floor.

From counter to door in less than 30 seconds

He's through that door in less than a nanosecond.

He doesn't need a menu and he's definitely barred

Oh yes - Chicks has been promoted to pigeon guard!

In he walks bold as brass expecting to be served

Ha not today my friend for you've been observed!

I've got my beady eyes on that bird

But he really does not seem deterred!

In fact I really think he is mocking me

One minute there's one - next there's three!

It's like he's gone off laughing and told all his mates

Come to this coffee shop and watch Chicks stacking plates

Then when she is fully loaded we'll just waddle in

Watch how she goes into a complete flat spin!

Oh you pesky, puffed up pigeons you may well laugh…

But it's about time you started leaving tips for the staff!

The Big Fat Seagull... King of Tenby

There is a great big fat seagull that sits outside the coffee shop
He sits and waits for any meagre crumbs that you may drop.

He doesn't walk, he doesn't fly - he merely waddles and sometimes hops
But don't be fooled because he is as wily as a fox.

He sits upon the old church wall and watches people passing by
And when he spies those chips or pasties only then does he fly.

From nowhere he appears and steals the unsuspecting victim's food
He's fast, he's silent, he's got perfect aim and is quite shrewd.

You open your mouth to sample your wares, bringing your delight up to your lips
Then poof - like magic - you suddenly have magic disappearing chips!

He swoops down in silence and devours what he caught.
All at once you look at your hands and there's nothing left of what you bought!

The king of Tenby never has to swipe his card or use hard earned cash!
The greedy seagull perches somewhere stealing the lot in a flash!

No time to chew, no posh table manners - down the hatch like a hole in one.
In less than thirty seconds this feathered fiend's dirty deed is done.

Once he's finished his fly by buffet he returns to his spot upon the wall.
It is here that you will hear him screech, squawk and bawl.

Crowing to all his bird like pals - another Greggs pasty has met its downfall!

The Pigeon's Demise

Well today saw the end of a beautiful relationship.
The end of what could have been a wonderful courtship.
A glorious day, the sun shining bright
Little did I know of the poor pigeon's plight!

I stroll to the coffee shop with not a care in the world
And there on the pavement, my pigeon, wings furled.
I say wings furled that's strictly not right
For I was met with a horrific sight!

My beautiful pigeon, who'd led me a merry dance
Well it looked like he hadn't stood a chance.
For there he lay and he was as flat as a pancake.
Probably diminished at the start of daybreak.

He'd probably been sat minding his own business
Maybe even looking forward to Christmas
But alas for it was just not meant to be.
No more pecking about under the church trees.

Gone in a moment - a very sad passing
Now there will be no more coffee shop trespassing.
So rest in peace my poor feathered friend
I only hope that it was quick at the end.

Faith & Reflections

The Here And Now

Without doubt

The sun will rise
The sun will set
The moon will come out
The stars will shine
The tide rolls in
The tide rolls out

All we have is the here and now.

Brexit Shaken Not Stirred!

We decided to leave the EU - there was a vote and it was go.
Brexit was on the cards - Cameron turned tail becoming the foe.
So we were out - run for the hills
No wait first stockpile all the pills!

Years of negotiations with European nations
I wish I had gone into hibernation.
Not before I'd stock piled some goods
Surely the media's not full of falsehoods?

Boris Johnson so full of promise
He and Nigel were oh so honest.
Now Nigel's walking north to south
With new nonsense coming from his mouth.

To hedge my bets I'm boxing clever
Over react - me - what - never.
I'm taking quite a serious stand
Stocked full of gin - it's really grand.

Now two years on the people are worn down
Mention Brexit and smiles turn to frowns.
Surely we must be nearly there
The mood is now full of despair.

I think I may just have the answer
We will send in an army of belly dancers.
The politicians would be distracted
And May could be quietly extracted.

But nobody really wants May's mission
Not even someone full of ambition.
She's really got the poisoned curse
And there's no going in reverse!

Let's turn off the lights and hunker down
Is the country being run by clowns?
Teresa May is pushing forward
Her manner generally quite awkward.

So here we are so much time has gone
And nobody has sounded the exit gong.
We best all just try and stick together
Remember the gin is dry whatever the weather!

VE Day 2020 - 75 Years On...

We gathered together as neighbours and friends
To celebrate 75 years since the war came to an end.
Seventy-five years - not many survivors are left
So many families were left sad and bereft.

We cannot really know the suffering they saw
At their bravery and resilience we look on in awe
Brave men and women who defended our land
Brave men and women following their commands.

We cannot imagine how hard it must have been
Leaving their loved ones, babies born but not seen.
They gave their lives so we could enjoy freedom
Giving us all our very own Garden of Eden.

Some left when they were not yet grown men.
Not knowing when they'd see their mothers again.
Fear swelling in their bellies but pride in their hearts
None of them knowing how long they'd be apart.

Some left their homes with a final goodbye
Went down the street, arms waving up high
People all cheering and wishing them good luck
Secretly hoping their loved ones wouldn't be struck.

Women and girls were called to work on the land
Keeping food aplenty for families left behind
The ladies produced weapons and ammunition
Knowing this was key to Great Britain's mission.

Sweethearts, wives and children - families torn apart
The pain of separation cutting deep into their heart.
Hugging their loved ones before they set off to war
Sadly some never came back through their front door.

1939 saw masses set off to defend our great country
Many thinking this battle would end most abruptly
But it raged on into 1945 - so many years - so many lives
Families bereaved losing sons, daughters, fathers and wives.

So 75 years on and we all gather to remember
Think of the loss of every family member.
But who knew we would be fighting again
But this time the enemy we fight is not men.

Our celebrations today marred by an invisible threat
This year that we are in - we won't ever forget.
As we sit and see pain, heartbreak and death
So many loved ones drawing their last breath.

The heroes of this war are our doctors and nurses
Fighting Covid-19 - one of mans greatest curses.
So today seems more poignant than ever before
For once again it's our freedom we must fight for.

A Glimmer Of Hope And Light

My breath pours out
Dancing in the cold air.
I sit, lonely and sad
In complete despair.

I look at my breath
As it leaves my mouth.
Hanging in the air
Ghost like floating about.

It's so cold I can't move
I can't feel my fingers or toes.
The saddest thing is I'm here
All alone - and nobody knows.

Sat in my sanctuary - my home
With windows that sparkle with ice.
You'd think it looks pretty
But with no heat - it's a sacrifice.

A tear falls from my eye
And I hang my head low.
What if I die here
And nobody knows.

My heart hurts so much
With pain I've not known.
Sat in one chair it's become
Like a poisonous throne.

I can't afford heat
And I can't afford food.
I sit and wonder
How would my life be viewed.

When we say the word home
It conjures an image of warmth.
Not a cold, lifeless place
Soulless and forlorn.

The silence is deafening
The TV a blank box.
Beyond that dark screen
An ironic paradox.

The light slowly fades
And I know it will get colder.
This isn't what I dreamt of
When I envisaged getting older.

As the darkness creeps
Across the icy cold room.
I know it's going to get
So much colder soon.

I clasp my hands together
And look up towards the Lord.
Praying for the heat
That I just can't afford.

If tonight is my last night
On this lowly earth.
I pray that my life
At least held some worth.

Darkness surrounds me
And the coldness is biting.
So I draw my freezing body
Under the blankets in hiding.

Please let me live
Survive this bitterly cold night.
Please let tomorrow
Bring a glimmer of hope and light.

The Bright Red Door

There's a house in a street that looks quite nice
To many it looks like a slice of paradise.
Your own home and your own front door
Who really wants much more?

You look at that house and it seems idyllic
An image of a perfect life it appears to mimic.
Behind the door of tranquil beauty
Are parents trying to perform their duty.

To look after their family both old and young.
Why does it feel like the government is holding a gun?
Behind the door painted a glorious bold red
A family whose days are filled with dread.

They wake up and put on a false smile
Underneath the masquerade they hide their lifestyle.
The family that's wrapping their whole family in love
Sat in desperate despair, as there's nothing left to get rid of.

They've sold what they can and they have nothing left
So now - what's left - they are left miserably bereft.
What's the problem I hear you ask?
What is it that the red door masks?

The house that looks like yours or mine
Is a household struggling as a result of our time.
A time where people are struggling and lost
Due to how much just ordinary living now costs.

So this family struggle but get up each day
Determine to face whatever comes their way.
But now they are facing life-changing choices
Do they realise that theirs are not lone voices?

Thousands of people doing a long, hard days toil
Yet they can't afford food, electricity or heating oil.
And what is it that we see the politicians doing
As our country is lying damaged and in ruins.

They lie and they squabble amongst themselves
Pointing fingers and blaming someone else.
Meanwhile people are starving and can't heat their homes.
It seems to some of us they have hearts made of stone.

So look at that house that seems idyllic and perfect
For them the good days gone by seem hard to recollect.
A country in turmoil with no sense of direction
PR gurus even given up with games of distraction.

So when you walk past somebody else's home
Remember what's going on inside is unknown.
We need to be kind and look out for one another
Someone struggling is somebody's mother, father, sister or brother.

The crisis we face may be too much for some to bear
So it's so important that we all show that we care.
Tonight someone's life may hang in the balance.
Unable to see light or a solution to the imbalance.

When the years have gone by many will sit and reflect
Who knows what will be the long term after effect.
So many are sat behind that bright red front door.
Not knowing what on earth lies in store.

Wasting Away

Choking - our seas and rivers
Are slowly choking.
Polluted and swamped
By humankind.

We profess to love animals,
To love the environment.
Yet our lives are surrounded,
By things we just throw away.

A disposable life,
Where nothing is treasured.
A second in our hands,
A lifetime in our seas.

We don't want the inconvenience,
Carrying a bag, a cup, a straw.
We walk this planet
With an air of a divine right.

Like humans are better,
Than any other living thing.
Easy come - easy go,
We are far too busy to care.

Meanwhile our waters,
Are littered with micro plastics.
Plastics filtering into the food chain,
Killing innocent creatures.

The damage is done,
The pollutants are out there.
Imagine being smothered,
By a man made material.

Only we can make the change,
Reduce our waste.
Care more about our planet,
All its living creatures.

Let's take a moment,
Stop and think.
If we had to keep all our waste,
Would we all create so much?

How Far Is It Between Earth And Heaven?

It's a long way between heaven and earth
You look up at the sky - I look back to your birth.
Above lies sky, clouds, stars, planets and moons.
Some places are only seen by a meteorological balloon.

Yes we can stand and admire heaven's night show.
As the stars and planets emerge and gently glow.
But what if the journey from earth to heaven
Is actually living and our daily life lessons.

It starts with your birth - the day you were born
Right until the moment from which there is no return.
Your life may long or it may be short
Lived alone or with lots of support.

So what is the journey from earth to heaven?
That is the lifelong unanswered question.
Most of us live every day in a mundane fashion
Some live life fast paced which oozes passion.

We constantly look to others for approval.
Other people's opinions seem to be crucial.
We can't seem to live life in our own lane.
Accepting the joys along with the pain.

Each day that breaks is another one of our journey
Some days are idyllic whilst some feel quite stormy.
But whatever the bumps in that lifelong road
We must keep on learning as our life unfolds.

So when we reach our life journeys end
And to our final resting place we do wend
Reflect on the path your life journey took you.
All that your mind, soul and body went through.

This marks the distance between earth and heaven
Your life should have felt like a special procession
So as you sit and reflect on your life today
Just remember to live life to the fullest, come what may.

We Live In A Beautiful World

We live in a beautiful world
Flowers hanging like pearls
Beautiful butterflies drifting on by
Birds soaring up in the deep blue skies

Creatures crawling and creeping around
Birds swooping making a choral sound
Lush green grass lies like a soft blanket
A medley of fresh flowers that you can cut

Trees standing tall like a century guard
Massive mountains making a picture postcard
Rivers that trickle, bubble and run
Sumptuous seas, waves glistening in the sun

Our human race is polluting its beauty
Protecting the environment is our duty
Suffocating the land and sea with plastics
When our world is beautiful and fantastic

Our human hearts, souls and minds
All intertwined and making us kind
Our eyes see the glory laid out before us
Humans are far from superfluous

We live in a beautiful world
And every day it's beauty unfurls.

A Hole In Your Soul

I saw a little piece of you fall away last night.
A tiny hole bored into your soul.

You weren't aware of this tiny crack opening up.
But I saw pain washing over you like a wave.

Life is closing in around you, creeping up silently.
Every day somehow feeling like it's a chore.

Every day another layer of sadness washing in.
Suffocating you and I see you fading away.

No light or happiness filtering in
Days feel like darkness and nights never ending.

I saw a little piece of you fall away last night
Let me help heal your soul and get you through this plight.

Letters To Heaven

If heaven could receive letters what would you say?
So much to say since the day you slipped away
I'd tell you that I'm doing fine and loving my life
It's not all been perfect - I've had my share of strife.

I feel like you've been watching me from afar
I'd often stand, look up and imagine you're a star
Our world stopped spinning on the day that you left.
At times my heart hurt so much I felt utterly bereft

But losing you made me stronger day by day
I was angry and full of pain that you couldn't stay
But time has past and now I see that no one lives forever
Our time was precious and I have memories to treasure.

I hope you are looking down and are proud of who I am
I will live a simple life and strive to be the best person I can
I will tell my grandchildren what a great person you were
You will live on in my heart and I feel you're always near.

Who Is Your Shepherd?

I wonder if we are all sheep just ambling along.
I wonder if we would follow any happy throng.
I wonder, if we are the sheep - then who the shepherd is.
I wonder if we'd all listen to all that shepherd says.

If you could follow anyone then who would you then chose?
If you could follow anyone would you pick who wore the nicest clothes?
If you could follow anyone would it be the one who spoke the loudest?
If you could follow anyone would you go where judgement seemed less clouded?

If you became the shepherd what message would you deliver?
If you became the shepherd would that just make you a giver?
If you became a shepherd would you make sure you included all the herd?
If you became a shepherd would you listen to all views no matter how absurd?

If you could pick your shepherd who would it be?
If you could pick your shepherd would it be for an eternity?
If you could pick your shepherd would you follow them devotedly?
If you could pick your shepherd would it be without negativity?

Whoever your shepherd may be then I hope they bring you a source of comfort.
Whoever your shepherd may be then I hope they were with you when you suffered.
Whoever your shepherd is then I hope you never feel lonely.
Whoever your shepherd is then I hope they are the one and only.

Faith - A Journey Of Trust

Lord, are you busy I think I'd like to chat.
I know that praying is something I'm not good at.
I never know what I'm supposed to say
In fact I'm not sure I know how to pray?

I think you are listening all the time.
To be honest that is absolutely fine.
But when it's down to just you and me
How do I know if you are even free?

Do I have to fall down on my knees?
I try but then my thoughts just freeze.
I feel a bit silly talking to myself.
I know it's a moment to find oneself.

There's been some bumps along the road.
At times it's felt like life may just implode.
Invisible chains choking all of my thoughts.
An army of hands tying my stomach in knots.

Darkness enveloping all my mind and soul.
Hopes and dreams being sucked into a black hole.
But Lord where were you in my time of need?
I thought you'd somehow intercede?

My child, do you think oxygen doesn't exist?
Air seeping in your body like a life-giving kiss.
You can't see it but you know that it's there.
I can and do interpret your silent prayers.

You thought I wasn't there in your darkest hours.
But I was there, up amongst the moon and stars.
I knew you had the strength to weather that storm.
Those hard times helped your heart and soul to form.

I silently guided you through those hard times.
You simply couldn't see all those reassuring signs.
Just open your heart, mind and soul.
Let words flow out like they're out of control.

I'm here for you child and will never let go.
Day by day your Christian faith will grow.
Like the air you can't see, I am wrapped around you.
Just remember to speak words, which are true to you.

Lord I think I now know how to pray
In you I have to trust and obey.
What you say - I will do.
Where you send me - I will go.

In you I trust and obey.

The Messenger From Heaven

I sit and stare intently
At the garden in full bloom
It's a place of pure beauty
It's where you come to roam

The serenity that surrounds me
Is pure and so divine
It washes and envelops me
It's like there is no time

There you sit and look at me
Your head tipped to one side
You hop, jump and walk about
Sometimes it's like you glide

You often stop in just one place
And I look into your eyes
I wonder if you are a gift from heaven
My mouth turns to a smile

You seem to sit for such a time
Just still and majestic
You live a very simple life
Where mine is very hectic

I reflect upon the paths we tread
And can see they are so different
Yours is all about surviving
Mine feels quite materialistic

I sense you are a messenger
From someone no longer here
I wish you could just hop up
And whisper in my ear

Something startles you
And you fly away
Mr Blackbird I do so hope
You will be back one day.

I Hope There Is A Heaven…

I hope there is a heaven,
above us in all its glory.

Somewhere that I can tell
my great life story.

A story of much joy
and happiness on the way.

Will the journey to heaven
be a glorious, liberating day?

High above the deep blue sky
beyond the stars and moon.

Lies a world wrapped in faith
where some go way too soon.

I hope there is a heaven
there for you and me.

Black Dog

Black dog, black dog you swarm into my life.
You creep in and swamp me,
And tape shut my mouth.
You dampen all feelings
And extinguish all joy.
You've blown a dark, joyless fog
Into all parts of mind.
When I look at my reflection
I don't recognise this vision.
Eyes full of despair,
I feel so lost and alone.
Black dog, black dog you swarm into my life.
An invisible blanket taking my life.

One Grain Of Sand

Time is precious
It slips through our fingers
As easy as grains of sand
And like the sand we don't appreciate it
One grain of sand on its own
What value has that?
One second in time
It's merely the blink of an eye
Put all those grains together
You have a glorious sandy beach
Put all the seconds of your life together
You have a lifetime of memories
But in just one second your whole life can change
Appreciate those seconds
They are as precious as that grain of sand

The Earth Has Quaked

How can we look in the mirror
And think that we need more?
When people across the globe
Have had their homes flattened to the floor.

They didn't see it coming, didn't stand a chance.
Buildings no longer standing in the worst circumstance.
People in their beds, now lie in concrete tombs.
These places that were once their safe living rooms.

Nature at its worst, we really cannot fathom.
Whole towns disappear into the earth's chasm.
Thousands lost their lives in a moment of horror.
Now death and destruction on every street corner.

So when you think you'd just like a bit more.
Be grateful that you live safely behind your own front door.
Let's spare a thought and pray for those suffering today.
Guide them through this time as we look on in dismay.

The Town That Is No More...

There once stood sanctuaries
Now reduced to rubble
What once was a bustling town
Now merely bricks, blocks and mortar

Nowhere safe to live or work
A community's history flatten to the ground
All in the name of war
A war raging on day by day

Children can no longer play in the street
No dogs playing freely in what was green space
A town a shadow of what it once was
All signs of life gone without trace

People living in fear
Displaced from their homes
Not knowing what their future may hold
So much loss and so much destruction

A war that still rages on...

People - Family, Friends And Life!

Dad

I thought I saw you standing there just the other day
I turned around to wave to you but you must have gone the other way.

I thought I smelt your aftershave as I walked down the street
I felt sure if I kept on walking we would be bound to meet.

I thought I heard your laughter rising up above the crowd
It truly felt it was just above me like a joyful bursting cloud.

I thought I heard your voice today as I went about my day
So many times I looked for you hoping I'd see you come what may.

I thought I felt your warm embrace wrap around my body
You used to give me cuddles despite me being stroppy.

I thought I sensed your presence as I rested in the sun
But then I came to realise I was not with anyone.

I know that you are with us as each second ticks on by
For you never really left us despite us saying goodbye.

I know that you are guiding us as you watch from far away
Willing us to succeed as we live our life each day.

I know that you are watching us and wishing you were here
With all the folk that loved you and held you oh so dear.

I thought I saw you standing there just the other day
So I looked up to the skies and gave you a great big wave.

Hide And Seek

I went to open the cupboard door
Now what was it I had come here for?
I scratched my head and pulled at my ear
Nope, still no idea why I was here.

I will walk away, that will work.
I'm beginning to feel a bit of a twerp.
I stroll around - looking down
Still the answer can't be found.

I know, I will try and retrace my steps
That's what always works the best.
Trouble is I'm not quite clear
From which of these rooms did I appear?

I will sit and have a cup of tea
Balance some biscuits on my knee.
I will forget about that blasted cupboard
It's making me feel like old Mother Hubbard.

It's so annoying don't you agree
When you can't recall things easily.
Perhaps I made a note somewhere
Now I'm starting to really despair.

Yes that will be it I will have written it down
You see, I'm not such a silly old clown.
Now where's my glasses - where could they be
I really must find them, as I do need to see.

Oh dear my poor memory is really quite testing
But I guess there's no point in standing protesting.
I know where I put them - of course - silly me
And now I remember - I needed to see.

So back to the cupboard I go with a stride
That says "woman on a mission" - so stand aside.
I open the cupboard door feeling triumphant
Oh look, a cheese sandwich smelling quite pungent!

I wondered what had happened to that gourmet delight
That I lovingly made just the other night.
Of course you know what this discovery means
My specs are in the fridge with yesterday's beans!

The River Of Life

Life is like a river
Wending its way down the steep mountain
It's pace often fast and turbulent,
At times nothing more than a mere trickle.

But down the mountain that rivers flows,
It seeks out its path and somehow gets through
It dances; it shimmers and gleams in the sun
At times it's so full as the rain bounces down
Other times its energy depleted and not all gets through.

The path that it follows is one that's well tread
So many droplets make up that great flow
A force of nature sometimes for the good
At other times destructive and a life changing flow.

Along its journey, water helps others to grow
The mosses and heathers dance along its banks
The fishes and animals who make this their home
Like a beating heart pulsing your lifeblood to all.

At some point in time that river or stream ends
Perhaps its final hurray over a wonderful waterfall
Or that clear sparkling water may join the great seas
No longer alone but in a mass of great glory.

So our lives are reflected in this mighty element
Some days are hard - others full of joy and happiness
At times it feels lonely but we try and get through
The end of the journey - who really knows?

But I hope there's a glorious end,
Like entering a great deep ocean, I'm joined in glory,
With the masses and those that I have loved.

In A World Where You Can Be Anything

In a world where you can be anything
Be kind

In a world where you can be anything
Be caring

In a world where you can be anything
Be thoughtful

In a world where you can be anything
Be generous

In a world where you can be anything
Be there

In a world where you can be anything
Be tolerant

In a world where you can be anything
Be fair

In a world where you can be anything
Be selfless

In a world where you can be anything
Be a listener

In a world where you can be anything
Be nice

In a world where you can be anything
Don't judge

In a world where you can be anything
Be you

The Glass Of Life

Do you ever feel that going through life is like watching that glass of water going down and down? Sometimes you think that you have reached the bottom of your glass, it feels like you are chasing the final drips around the bottom of the glass - desperately trying to make those tiny droplets quench your thirst for life. Some days it just feels like the glass is so full of emptiness it will never be full of life again.

Then when we least expect it something comes along and fills that glass back up - life and living - that's what fills that glass back up. People and laughter - that's what fills that glass back up. Loving and feeling loved - that's what fills that glass back up. Giving more than you receive in life that's what fills that glass back up. Being in the moment helps us to evaluate those hard bumps in the road of life - sometimes the bumps are so big we may never get over them, always feeling like we are climbing up them, alone and feeling lonely. But sit back - look around - reach out - often you realise you are never really alone. Someone or something comes along that makes you appreciate you may be feeling lost in that moment but there is often a hand and a heart reaching in to gently pull you out.

It will be those small things in life - the things that just make you stop and smile for a moment - these things make us appreciate where we are.

I know that sometimes the glass is cracked or chipped and may never feel full again - but those moments are there that will help fill your glass up. Life is strange - if you ever feel like your glass is running dry don't despair human nature is such that it will fill up again. If you want to help fill up the glass of life do some random acts of kindness - you will be surprised what a difference it can make. That gesture can sometimes be all that person needed to know that somebody cares about them.

So try it - see if you can replenish the glass - it doesn't matter if it's yours, mine or someone else's - turn on the tap of life and let it flow come what may.

She Danced

She danced like her heart depended on it
She danced like she was all alone
She danced like a free spirit
She danced like she was wearing her soul on the outside
She danced and all her worries melted away
She danced - simply because she could

Your Invisible Cape

I wear an invisible cape
Most of us do.
Some know they have it
And it's been their life glue.

My cape doesn't mean
That I'm a superhero.
It can take me at top speed
But then drop down to zero.

It's a sad state of affairs
That not all capes are equal
And our early roots
Can determine our sequel.

Society can also dictate
The shape and fit of our cape.
Forcing many to wear capes
That don't fit their shape.

Some people are lucky
And get a cape and passion.
Some capes are heavy
And cannot be unfastened.

The design of your cape
Is set early on
But it doesn't have to be
The one that you don.

I can see you looking
On most perplexed.
I can see that I've not
Shared my pretext.

This invisible cape I refer to
Is your education.
But don't think it's just
From birth to graduation.

Each day we start anew
New day and new dawn
Opportunities for learning
To keep us moving on.

So never think
It's just too late for me.
Remember education is vital
And can help turn that key.

You've Got This

Don't worry I've been where you've been.
I've felt all those feelings you are feeling.
I've nursed a broken heart.
I've felt pain so deep I could barely breath.
I've walked every step with you.
Been here for you.
But so often you dismissed me.
Didn't notice me.
I quietly picked up the pieces.
I knew we'd be able to put them back together.
Maybe not today.
Maybe not tomorrow.
But once you were strong again.
I knew we'd fix you.
I always had faith in you.
You never believed in that faith.
But that didn't stop me from having that faith.
I am your safety net.
Your constant.
Your guide.
Your confidant.
My eyes bore into yours.
I implore you to believe you are strong.
You've got this.
You can do anything.
I look deep into your soul.
See your scars.
Feel your hurt.
Lived through your healing.
Look harder.
You are looking at your greatest power.
You.

You take one more glance into the mirror.
I smile back at you.
You've got this.

Reclaim Your Youth - Be Brave!

I am going in come what may
Heading straight into that sea spray.
My belly rounded and thighs wobbling
Feet look like they belong to a goblin!

But do you know what I do not care
So what if my body is like a conference pear?
It has served me well - I can't complain
So I am sorry if it causes you eye strain!

It is not about how you look
Those supermodels in those books.
Not real women like you and me
So come on ladies - hear my plea.

Just get out there - go and do it
Don't ever feel like some misfit.
It is your body - it serves a function
All it takes is a bit of gumption.

Take the plunge and set yourself free
Run girl run right into the sea.
Let the waves wash right over you
Despite the fact you are turning blue!

Now don't you feel oh so good?
Reclaiming your lost girlhood.
See never think you are some has been
Now go and pour a great big gin!

The Scars Of Life

You are not broken.
You display the scars of life.
When you are at your lowest,
The pain you feel,
Will shape the future you.
You are not broken
You are growing
Day by day.

What Is Ordinary?

I am just an ordinary girl.
Plain, simple ordinary girl.
I am nothing special.
I am not extraordinary.
I am just an ordinary girl.

We live in a very ordinary world.
Surrounded by nature.
It's nothing special.
Hemmed in by buildings.
It's not extraordinary.
We live in a very ordinary world.

But what is ordinary?
What does ordinary mean?
Is anyone just ordinary?
Maybe we are all extraordinary?

Look at our bodies.
Take a moment to think.
Bodies which adapt.
Bodies which heal.
Bodies that do incredible things.
So surely nobody is "ordinary".

Look at the world.
It's full of creation.
From the tiniest creature.
To mountains that seem to meet the universe.
Adapting and changing to its ever-changing environment.
Surely this is no ordinary world.

We are all extraordinary.
We live in an extraordinary world.
So when you feel worthless and small.
Remember your body is a miracle.
You are its owner so that makes you extraordinary.

Child's Play

Everything is new and needs exploring
No minute is dull and no day is boring.
Every surface feels suspiciously strange
But not everything is yet in my range.
What's over here? I am very curious
Whatever it is, it looks rather glorious.

Oh but here we go I'm being pulled up
Mum has come along and my game is up.
As hard as I try I never quite get there
Mum is always there telling me to beware.
But everything looks so exciting and tempting
I don't understand why she's trying to protect me.

As I toddle around I seek out new items
But wherever I trundle my mum is always frightened.
As soon as I pick up that object to lick
She's taken it off me - darn that woman is slick.
We went out with the dogs for a little walk
How did I know you are not meant to eat leafstalks?

We went to this place called a beach
I was soon just out of my mum's reach.
I look at the substance beneath my feet
Wow that looks pretty, good enough to eat.
I grab at a handful of those tiny grains
In my mouth I pop it mmm it sure is strange.

It's gritty, hard and crunchy as well
I'm thinking I will also lick my seashell.
I bring the shell up towards my mouth
Before I know it mum has pulled it out.
She's shouting again, sometimes she's no fun
I think this could be my cue to just run!

At home mum has things she calls candles
I like to chew them but she thinks that's a scandal!
She's up out her chair and like that, it's gone
Here she goes, she's going to ramble on
I mustn't eat that they don't taste nice
She's pleading with me to follow her advice.

Her advice is so boring as I mustn't touch this
She goes on and on and then she wants a kiss!
I really don't get it, this woman filled with love
As she's tutting and moving candles way up above.
I don't understand why she's spoiling my fun.
I think I may win this game in the long run.

I sit and stare at the array of toys
They are colourful and lots make a noise.
I glance around the room so much to explore
That's without what lies beyond that door.
I will just post my toys through that slot I can see
Oh man, here's my mum and once again she disagrees.

Apparently toys must go away in "the box".
My cars, the trains, the teddies and blocks.
I'm not to put them under the settee
And apparently the toilet doesn't "set them free".
So many rules I just don't understand
Sometimes I just scream and lie on the ground.

But my mum smooth's my hair and kisses my head
She gently tells me the days done and it's time for bed.
I am rather tired, it's hard work being an explorer
Maybe tomorrow it will all seem much clearer.
I do seem to learn a little bit more each day
Wow it's really hard work this child's play!

Battle Lines Are Drawn

You stand defiant
Not moving a muscle
You think you are a giant
I know you're on a hustle

The battle lines drawn
I firmly fold my arms
You've not got the brawn
I won't weaken to your charms

Suddenly a change of tact
A smile sweeps across your face
I feel my resolve crack
You've innocently played your ace

Please nana please
Like butter wouldn't melt
You've won again with ease
Now a hug that's heartfelt

I give up, I give in
Alright I will get the biscuit tin!

That Old Jumper

As you go through life you accumulate things
Accumulate, accumulate, accumulate
Clothing, jewellery, books, ornaments, photos
Material things
Accumulate –
But you also accumulate people
Forge friendships over time
People - like clothing in our wardrobe
We keep adding to the wardrobe
Adding, adding, adding
The wardrobe gets fuller and fuller
And that once cherished jumper gets pushed further and further back
You now no longer wear it - but yet you can't let it go
You pick it up, hold it and a flood of memories wash over you
You remember that trip to the theatre, the time you fell over out walking
The time you were told a loved one had died, the time your new puppy lay on it
A garment, a thing, an item but yet you feel an emotional attachment to it
So you see people can feel like that clothing
We travel through life, along our path meeting lots of people as we go
Some we try on for size and the fit is just not right
So many others we have a strong bond with but as time passes it lessens
You don't love them any less but with all the new things entering your life
They slowly ebb further away
But yet when you think of them your heart is full of joy
So many good times and memories that your cherish
So whilst you may no longer see them regularly you still hold them dear
So like that beautiful faithful old jumper you still want it in your life
Because you know that you could just pick it back up and it would still fit just right.

Wet Pants

When did we get so miserable?
Charging down the street
Just get out of my way
You're not someone I want to meet.

Darn it now the rain has come
Large drops are running down my nose
Oh jeepers I can even feel it
Seeping slowly around my toes!

Now I'm soaked right through
Even my brassière is feeling damp
Oh great my hairs a mess
And now I just feel like a tramp.

Now I've two great big panda eyes
Where mascara once did sit
This stupid weather
Makes you feel really…

Oh wait a minute
I think I spy a rainbow
Arching over the clouds up high
Well I guess I don't feel quite so low.

When did we get so miserable?
And moan at everything
I mean surely every day
I'm grateful for at least one thing.

I stand and tap my foot and tut
When I'm stood in a queue
I'm even known to roll my eyes
And I'm bound to need the loo.

My patience is at zero
As there are places I need to be
I'm a very busy person
I've no time for this can't you see.

Whilst we are busy being miserable
And rushing here and there
There's a whole world out of the window
If we'd just stop and stare.

Sit back a moment and watch a child
You'll soon see what I mean
For their world is new and sparkly
And there's so much they haven't seen.

When that rain was running down my nose
The children were just laughing
They jumped in puddles and splashed around
For to them the rain was quite cathartic.

Bring a child an ice cream
You'll see their eyes open wide
Like you'd offered them the Crown Jewels
And a diamond they had spied.

Bring a child some chocolate cake
They will think they've died and gone to heaven
Add some squirty cream and sprinkles
Well - there's a life lesson.

For a child finds pure joy
In the simplest of things
They are not interested in
Money, cars or huge diamond rings.

Present them with some bubbles
And you've got a happy child
Watch those bubbles float away
And all they can do is smile.

When did we get so miserable?
Dashing here and there
Do you know that rain has reached my pants
And now I really do not care!"

It's Friday! It's Friday!

It's Friday! It's Friday!
Let's do a little dance!
It's Friday! It's Friday!
Let's all stand up and prance!

It's Friday! It's Friday!
The Merlot is waiting.
It's Friday! It's Friday!
Time for hibernating.

It's Friday! It's Friday!
Cwtch under a blanket.
It's Friday! It's Friday!
Lay out a chocolate banquet!

It's Friday! It's Friday!
Light the scented candles.
It's Friday! It's Friday!
Forget the economic shambles.

It's Friday! It's Friday!
Switch off that alarm.
It's Friday! It's Friday!
Weekend work your charm.

Wrinkly, Crinkly Skin...

Oh nana why is your skin all wrinkly and thin?
Ah, I say, it's because my body is well lived in.
Well I don't want to have skin that's all wrinkly
Like a chip that's not smooth but actually all crinkly!
Did you sit out in the rain for too long?
Or was it because your skin isn't strong?
I don't understand how my skin is smooth
Come on nana I want to hear the truth!

Well child what you must remember
Is that each of these lines represents a memory.
I've lived a good long life you see,
I hope you live as long as me!
Oh but nana you are mega old and been around forever
That's why you are so wise and clever.
But why couldn't you stop your skin from shrinking?
You maybe got it wet too much - that's what I'm thinking.

No child that's not the reason for the folds and creases
You see over time our body generally gets weaker.
These deep-seated lines are like my battle scars,
If you like, it's a visual reminder of all my memoirs.

It's an honour to sport such lines as these.
But nana you've even got them on your knees!
Remember it's not the body that makes a person
A lesson that you must never stop learning.
Yes my skin is no longer soft and smooth
But listen carefully while I tell you the truth.
Your body gets slower and yes your skin may shrink!
I hate to tell you that it may not even stay rosy and pink.

But think of your body like your home
Look after it as through life you roam.
For you will learn one day that YOU are your heart and soul.
Your heart, mind and soul are what you can truly control.
Stay true to you and always be grateful and kind,
You don't want to reach the end without any lines!

So nana, lines are like medals like you win in races
Except these appear on our arms, legs and faces.
We should be proud that our skin is creased
It's not that we should have kept it well greased!
Yes like your beautiful home you must look after it well
But your soul is inside like that pearl in the oyster shell.
So live, love and laugh and reach for the stars,
Spread kindness and joy and you will go far!

Life - The Tapestry We Weave

As you go along your life
A picture you will weave.
We only see the finished image
When we are left - bereaved.

Every moment passing by
Is a stitch into that picture.
Every breath you take,
The image grows by just a flicker.

Every time you stop and smile
At someone in the street.
A connection's made, a stitch put in
For all those people that we meet.

Lives entwined
And yet time spent apart.
But that person
Becomes embedded in your heart.

As time passes along its road
We connect a little less.
But there's still a piece of my heart
Locked away for you nevertheless

Suddenly it's months not weeks
That we've not really spoken.
And now there's a lifetime
That will remain unspoken.

You were never really
Very far from my thoughts.
Even more so, as we now try
And comprehend this pain and loss.

Your tapestry left unfinished
So many more stitches to go in.
Now your beautiful family
Continue the story herein.

A smile that lit up a room
A laugh that was infectious.
Taken from us just too soon
Memories now so precious.

Know that your were loved
By so many that you met.
Our friendship and our time together
Are things that I will never forget.

In loving memory of a beautiful friend.

Me Time - Never Feel Guilty About It!

Is there anything more important than self-care?
Don't ever underestimate the need to sit and share.
Life's journey can beat a dark, lonely path at times.
Darkness wrapping around your body sometimes.
Desperately seeking out any tiny chink of light.
Fighting waves of feeling lost and being out of sight.
Cold, clammy invisible hands gripping round your throat.
Afraid to talk and feeling completely out of sorts.
Everybody needs to know that there is someone there.
Some organisation, friend or stranger who can show they care.

So if you are feeling completely lost or simply overwhelmed.
If you just simply want a warm embrace or to be held.
Take that moment to stop, listen, look and breathe.
Strip away the dark thoughts, as there is hope underneath.
So take some time for the important things.
I don't mean clothes, makeup, shoes and fancy rings.
YOU - are the most important thing in your life.
Seek out help to deal with feelings and any strife.
Know that have such amazing self worth.
You are the most important thing on this earth.
So don't ever feel guilty for having "me" time.
Life's an interesting mountain we all must climb.

Tomorrow Without You

I wish I had a superpower, anything would do.
So long as my superpower meant I could save you.
I never knew you were hurting and in so much pain.
That your worries were drowning you like never ceasing rain.

I didn't read the signs that were so clearly there.
I hate the fact that you may think I didn't really care.
I can't imagine what each hour was like, day to day.
I feel so angry that there are things we can never say.

I will never understand what drove you to those lengths.
I wish I could have helped you increase your inner strength.
I wish I was like superman and I'd have taken to the skies.
Turning the world backwards as round the earth I'd fly.

I'd give anything to go back in time and hold you in my arms.
If you'd let me in I could have helped you through the storms.
I have a suffocating pain in my chest like nothing I've ever felt.
It tightens around my neck, gripping tightly like a belt.

At times I'm filled with anger at the decision that you took.
If only I'd realised that your life wasn't an open book.
I thought that I knew you and you'd always be right there.
Now I'm left with a gaping hole and feeling such despair.

I wish I had a superpower, anything would do.
If only it meant I could spend one more day with you.
And help ease the pain that you were wading through.
Now I'm left with facing all the tomorrows without you.

You Chose To Cross The Final Bridge

Just like that you were gone.
I don't know how I can carry on.
As quick as it takes to flick a switch.
You chose to go over your final bridge.

In an instance all our lives changed.
We are left - feeling alone and estranged.
You woke up and decided you could take no more.
Why couldn't you see how much you were cared for?

Feelings of anger surge through my body.
You just checked out and left everybody.
I'm searching to understand how you felt.
Despair and hopelessness at the hand dealt?

I'm grieving for such an enormous loss.
Waves of sadness and anger, I feel so cross.
I'd give anything to just turn back the clock.
So I could sit with you and we'd just talk.

What can be so bad that you chose this route?
For you to look at your life and decide to check out.
I feel my tears slowly rolling down my cheeks.
This simple emotion, yet volumes it speaks.

I want to scream and shout out loud.
I feel so alone even when sat in this crowd.
Alone with my thoughts and unanswered questions.
If you'd have talked it through I'd have made suggestions.

I was there for you, I was on your side.
What was it that made your world collide?
Collide and implode with some deep dark secret.
That sent you spiralling into a deep dark rut.

I can't stop these tears from falling from my eyes.
I should really be sat here full of hate and despise.
I will never understand why you did what you did.
Your sadness and despair you cleverly hid.

I will cherish our memories of all the good times together.
Who knew I'd soon just be left with memories to treasure.
As quick as it takes to flick a switch.
You chose to go over your final bridge.

That Song

That song; that song I keep hearing
It dances across the room into my ears
I hear it everywhere and sadness comes and hits me
Like a punch to my stomach
Bang!
That song
The song they played when we had to say our goodbyes
Too soon
Unexpected
My heart is squeezed so hard like it's in a vice
Suddenly I can't breathe
Thoughts sent into a swirling whirlpool of memories
A tear slowly rolls down my cheek
Followed by another
Cascading down my face - it's salty wetness against my skin
Like a waterfall dropping into nowhere
I wipe the tears away
My cheeks still wet - glistening in the evening sun
That song
The song that will forever remind me of you
The day we had to say goodbye.

Reflections Of You...

I'm staring deeply, intently into the water.

The water - dark with an unknown depth to it.

Yet it has a clean mirror like sheen.

Still – but moving.

I can almost see myself looking back

A distorted vision of me.

Distorted by the ripples that gently move across it

It's me but it's not me.

Water reflecting back at me.

Is this how the world sees me?

Is this how I see myself?

Do any of us know the real person inside of us?

Or are we merely reflecting ourselves to the world.

Reflecting what we think we should.

Reflecting what "society" makes us feel we should.

Reflecting who we think we should be.

I smash my fist down into the icy cold water.

Droplets of water disperse the image.

I'm no longer there...

I'm there – but in pieces.

The ripples lessen and the water calms.

Once again I can see my reflection.

I sit and ponder...

Who am I - why are we here - what does it all mean.

Despite the water moving, my reflection stays.

A changing image as the water flows onwards.

It seems to know its path, no faltering - just moving forward.

Yet we face so many paths, so many decisions.

Like the flowing water we move forwards,

But we look backwards.

Like the water smashing into rocks - we find another route when our options feel blocked.

Ever questioning ourselves - always doubting our moves.

We need to be as certain as the water.

We need to not look back.

Just move forward.

And remember...

That reflection is just one of our many layers.

It's OK to have a face for the outside world.

But always be happy in your heart and soul.

Always be content with what you portray.

Be you.

That reflection is just one image of you.

Like that spontaneous photo - another image.

And like the reflection we are ever changing.

Ever changing - with an unknown depth inside us.

Never doubt your abilities or worth.

We all have a purpose - like the water.

We are the lifeblood of society and our communities.

So just be you - be content - be kind - be inclusive

But most of all - believe in you.

Touch It - Feel It - No Live It

How do we measure success?

Can we touch it?
Can we feel it?
Can we count it?

Are we born with it?
Are we taught it?
Are we oblivious to it?

Do we need it?
Do we want it?
Do we have to have it?

Should we aspire to it?
Should we achieve it?
Should we be grateful for it?

Could we fake it?
Could we lose it?
Could we live without it?

Who decides what it is
Who judges if you've achieved it
Who cares?

There is only one thing you need to know

It's YOUR success
YOUR measure
YOUR goals
YOUR ambitions
Only YOU can judge YOUR success

What is a major achievement for one could be an insignificant moment in another person's life. What may seem trivial to you may be a huge milestone for someone else.

So let's not judge each other - let's just be kind - let's just be compassionate- let's just be nice - let's celebrate the small things -

let's not put others down - success is personal - it can be public - it can be private - you may feel like it's never going to happen - but it already has because you are here reading this and alive - just living is the greatest gift we can have.

Riches Of Life

Dear God

I know you don't hear from me much
You may say we are out of touch
But I'm struggling and need a friend
Someone to help my broken heart mend.

I have no money and I have no hope
It's hard day to day just to cope.
"My child, what's the problem - I'm always here.
Don't worry, speak freely and with no fear."

My children just need more and more.
Every day feels like a huge chore.
"My child, what is that your children need?"
So much it makes my sad heart bleed.

"My child, don't get sad and so upset.
You've lived a life with no regret."
But I can't give my children what they want.
Their friends have started to mock and taunt.

"My child, I ask you to open your eyes.
Look beyond just the immediate skies."
I don't understand what is it that you mean.
"I mean look beyond what it is you've seen."

"Do your children have food in their belly?
They don't go around dirty and smelly.
Do they sleep with a roof over their head?
Have they got their own cosy bed?"

Well yes Lord, they do have those things.
But it's the other things pulling at my heartstrings.
They want the latest games and mobile phone
They want new toys and a flying drone.

They want the latest designer clothes.
I can barely ensure theirs have no holes.
"My child, open your eyes and look wider.
You really are their steady, reliable provider."

I really don't understand what you mean?
Look beyond what I have seen?
"My child, do you really think you are poor?
Because you do not live a life of grandeur?"

"Riches aren't made up of money in the bank.
Your life is so rich, it's not dark and dank.
You have a roof above your head.
Children asleep in their own bed."

"Your family is safe, dry and warm.
You keep them away from any harm.
You all have your health and each other.
Surely this makes you the best mother?"

"You may feel poor and inadequate.
You really mustn't feel second rate.
Look beyond your own small horizon.
In other countries there are those barely surviving."

"Riches come from deep within your heart.
Shelter, warmth, food - that's a great start.
Some children in the world have none of this.
Some have nothing, roaming streets, motherless."

"So give thanks for the good things in your life.
There are always others with more trouble and strife.
There will always be others who have so much more
But remember there are those who are truly poor."

Are You There?

If I reach my fingers up to the sky can I touch you?
If I lift up my face will I feel your glory wash over me?
If I open my eyes wide like two wondrous pools of hope
Will I see you?
If I open my hands like expanses of land will I feel your touch?
I tilt my head back and I'm bathed in sunshine, pouring over my
   face like a child pours water from a bucket
I sense you are near
I feel your presence
It's like I feel your spirit enveloping all of my body
A reassuring hug
Yes if I reach my fingers up to the sky I know you are there.

Open Your Soul

Wear your soul on the outside
Make other people smile
Show off your soul with pride
Send negativity into exile

Your soul is your invisible power
When we die our souls are no more
Like when petals fall from the flower
Or the sea rolls back from the sandy shore

We are our souls, whole and true
We're not our physical bodies
The universe is calling out to you
So be you, don't be carbon copies

Set your soul free to soar and grow
Listen to those voices in your head
You have inner beauty to put on show
So open your soul - let happiness spread

Sands Of Time

Your hand in mine
The sands of time
Are slowly slipping away
Please don't go - stay

Your body lying there
Your eyes just stare
Stare up at that bleak ceiling
I don't know what you are feeling

Your motionless body barely breathing
My warm hand you are squeezing
A gentle squeeze
I try to put you at ease

You are not with us
And now you make no fuss
You almost look at peace
Knowing that your life will cease

Time, it doesn't stand still
Now delivering a bitter pill
We cannot stop it
Not even just a tiny bit

It's not really you in that bed
So much left unsaid
Your final hours in this world
Your fingers around mine - curled

I think of the good times we had
Memories swirling; good, funny and sad
Taken away by this vile virus
Now it is death you desirous

Too young to be taken
I'm willing you to awaken
I feel your grip slowly loosen
Slipping away like a setting sun

Your hand in mine
Losing against the sands of time
I will sit with you my friend
Stay close with you to the end

The Deep Grip Of Grief

Grief you swarm in suffocating every emotion.
Like a dark substance you silently creep everywhere.
Seeping through every part of my mind and body.
Clouding everything- removing all feelings.
Leaving me numb.
Pain crawling up from the pit of my stomach.
Your grip around my throat is so tight.
I cannot speak.
I cannot breathe.
I cannot think.

You swept in like someone in a rage.
Turning everything in my life upside down.
Nothing makes sense anymore.
Everything seems pointless.
A deep fog swirling around my mind.
I can't see.
I can't hear.
I can't feel.
Life changed forever.

I sit alone in the darkness.
I don't want other people's comfort.
Other people's kind words.
Other people's warm embrace.
Other people want to hug my pain away.

It feels like there is no point in continuing.
Without you.
My rock.
My anchor.

Days feel endless.
Like there's no beginning or end.
I feel as if my feet are in concrete blocks.
Every step is an effort.
Every word forced out of my mouth.
My mouth that was once filled with laughter.

I wake up.
Another day ahead of me.
I look towards the window.
I stare at the light forcing its way through the tiniest gap.
I think if that light can find a way to shine through that tiny gap, surely I can find the strength to live my life.
I look at the shard of light, falling onto the carpet.
I track its root - amazed how far that small beam reaches.
I wonder if my life has been as wide reaching.
I look at the sunlight shining in and notice how when it bounces off other objects it changes.
Beautiful lilacs, pinks, yellow, gold and green
It's fascinating that one chink can touch so much.

In that moment I realise that I still have so much to offer.
So many other lives that I can help.
I can shine my light into their world.
In their darkness I can help be their light.

I smile - I sense you are nearby.
I sense you are telling me "you can do this"
I sense that I still have a purpose.
This is a new chapter in my life.

As I start to heal I feel the dark grip of grief lessen its hold on me.
I know that the grief will never leave me - it's part of me - some days it may be all of me but other days I will be that chink of light and spread my rainbow of hope to others.

Shine Like A Star

Millions of stars - but yet no two the same.
Stars that glisten, like a sparkly hall of fame.

Look up at that night sky one cold, dark night.
It really is quite an extraordinary sight.

A gallery of diamonds and it's all completely free.
The same view from gardens, mountains and the sea.

Look up in awe, as it's a sight taken for granted.
It's a mystery laced with a touch of enchantment.

The stars and planets should keep us grounded.
When you think there are too many to even be counted.

What lies out there in those dark galaxies?
Stars and planets giving rise to many fantasies.

Nobody knows what lies beyond black holes.
Though we send up rockets like exploring moles.

Galaxy upon galaxy littered with gleaming stars.
Dwarfing this humble small world of ours.

When darkness descends the skies come alive
No motive, no agenda, no burning desire to thrive.

Their beauty is simple and there lies the key.
A life lesson for you and for me.

Just wake up each day and shine bright like that star.
Remember everyone has a part to play whoever they are.

A Glass Of Wine Is Just Fine!

I'd rather like my life to be like a glass of red wine
Rich, dark and full and enjoyed over a long time.
Full of lots of varieties and maybe even spice
The ability to transport me to a wondrous paradise
Yes I'd rather like my life to be like a glass of wine.

Loneliness

Loneliness - a silent killer that creeps from nowhere
Suffocates your heart and mind
Left feeling that life is no longer kind
All that you are left with is just you and your prayers.

Loneliness - where did you crawl from in all your glory?
Ripping the soul from my beautiful life
I once was somebody's wonderful wife
Memories swimming all around now feeling like a story

Loneliness - nobody knows how quietness is not want you want to hear
Surrounded by silence - no escape
Your only view a Constable landscape
Remember when your house was full of loved ones who you held so dear

Loneliness - your fingers creeping slowly up my neck to stifle the air I breathe
Sat remembering happier days gone by
A houseful of people and full of joy
My house once my castle has become my prison and that just makes me seethe.

Loneliness - how can you come in and make my once full life feel so empty
I've photos around me of days gone by
My family now gone but there's been no goodbyes
Living their lives to the fullest they can, leaving the nest in their early twenties.

Loneliness - something I never dreamt would slide into my beautiful home
Every day the same - sat all alone
My precious family are all fully grown
My job done as my loved ones spread their wings and are starting to roam.

Loneliness - I won't let you consume my every waking hour and suck out all my hope
I've lived a full life and I'm thankful for that
It's nobody's fault my home is becoming my trap
So I will take the mantle and strive to bring joy and help any others trying to cope.

A Broken Mind

I hear you've broken your arm.
How on earth did you come to such harm?
Are you in pain? Does it hurt very much?
How annoying, you can't grip or even touch.

I hear you've twisted your ankle.
Fell over and landed at the wrong angle.
I can see how hard it is for you to walk.
I'm here if you want to just sit and talk.

I hear you slipped and broke a rib.
How on earth did you manage to trip?
I can see the pain you are in as you breathe.
You are doing it through gritted teeth.

I hear you took a nasty tumble.
You've every right to moan and grumble.
I can see that awful cut on your arm.
You rest up and stay nice and warm.

I hear that she just sits around.
Miserable face with a deep-seated frown.
She never wants to sit and chat.
I can't be bothered with any of that.

I'm trapped within my own head.
Some days I just lay on my bed.
My mind is broken but nobody knows
You see broken minds just don't show.

I try and get out of these four walls.
Sometime I just can't answer my calls.
So I sit and watch the clock - tick tock.
If only I had someone who'd just sit and talk.

Mental health is invisible to you and I.
So if someone is aloof maybe ask yourself why.
Physical injuries are so clear to see.
A broken mind could happen to you or me.

My Sexy Beau…

Oh hello you devil - it's lovely to see you
If you hadn't arrived I'd have felt a bit blue!
You snuck up behind me all of a sudden
Don't spoil it now by making me go running.

You are quite possibly my most favourite thing.
Although I know it's just a brief fling.
We will sing, we will dance and maybe drink wine
You know when you are here it's always divine.

You have two sides and I really quite like it
The first half is my favourite I have to admit.
It's all about wine and no need to diet
Then you slow down and become a bit quiet.

As time moves on you look so serene
A gentler pace but you do mean we clean.
There's no escape from that duster and mop
And George is around and he's playing bad cop!

So if you ask me my favourite - which half I prefer?
Why I'd have to pick Saturday's although it's sometime a blur!
I do love the Sunday's all lazy and slow...
My best friend the weekend - you darn sexy beau.

Words

Words, words, words tumbling out of our mouths
Free, freely, for we have freedom of speech.
Some meaningful, others meaningless.
They roll out of our mouths floating across the air
Listened to, heard, misheard, reacted to.

Words, words, words used too much - used too little
Hatred, love, despair and grief
Emotive, emotional, insincere, heartfelt.
They connect us - are an expression of us.
They separate us and cause great divides.

Words, words, words they shape our lives
Hourly, daily, weekly, monthly, a lifetime.
Forgotten, forgettable, memorable, never forgotten.
They create moments, shape events, change events
We are what comes out of our mouths,
Whether it's spoken, written, signed, expressed.

Words, words, words they can map out our futures
Intimate, enemies, families, strangers, political, global.
Loud, soft, harsh, tender, sung, sobbed.
An outlet of how we feel, what we believe
A map, a guide to a greater understanding of you, me, everyone

Use them wisely
Use them kindly
Use them often
Use them carefully
Use them from your heart

Your words can shape other peoples lives.

A Snapshot In Time...

Click, click, click - life captured in a moment
Instant videoing that just keeps on rolling.
Media available at the tip of your finger
Creating memories that will forever linger.

What would we recall without these aide memoirs,
Would memories just fall into our minds reservoirs?
Photos capture a moment - a second in time
Autumn, winter, summer and springtime.

All seasons, all times - even our emotions
Stories told but where words are unspoken.
A picture that can depict happy family moments
But what if a beautiful life should be sadly stolen.

These photos stir up a range of different emotions
As humans, grief leaves us in pain and broken.
Photos suddenly take on a whole different value
Precious moments, which stand static in time.

That moment we captured may have felt almost meaningless
But years down the road we view them with fondness.
That view that you love or achieving your goals
Reliving the good times is good for your souls!

So keep snapping memories and store them away
For that simple photograph may be priceless one day.
A document of a life that shaped who you became.
Capturing the pleasure, happiness, laughter and pain.

So keep snapping away wherever you go
For one day that photo may be all you can view.

Seasons

Weightless Delicate Delight

Have you ever sat and watched snowflakes falling
It's a magical show and truly enthralling.
They glisten like glitter as they fall through the air
Spontaneously dancing and prancing without a care.

Each snowflake bears its own unique form
With the wind beneath them they swirl and swarm
Floating freely like weightless, delicate delights.
A true thing of beauty as winter bites.

They fall in slow motion from the darkened sky.
Then drop to the ground where it's here they lie.
Flake after flake 'til a white crisp blanket is formed.
Now the ground has a bright white coat to adorn.

The white fresh snow glistens and gleams
It's almost like walking through a dream.
Everywhere falls into a beautiful silence
Except for the birdsong calling out like a siren.

Nature's wonderland all now a pure white
It is a gloriously simple but stunning sight
But slowly and surely all life starts to move
Children playing and cars finding their groove.

Before long the perfect pure blanket is gone.
Where children, dogs, birds and adults walked on.
The remnants of a day of laughter and fun
And now the winter snow filled day is done.

Spring - A Lifetime Away...

Beauty cascading all around
Bluebells flourishing deep
In an unknown woodland.
Nature is evolving day by day.
The trees branches reaching upwards
Towards the sunlight, streaming and dancing
Through its branches as it pours downwards.
Branches laden with leafy glory.

The delicate pure white snowdrops
Are beginning to fade away
Each petal hides an inner glory.
Fallen leaves now lay
Like a mulch like brown carpet
The goodness from the end if it's life
Feeding the new soils deep below.

On the branches buds peep out
New leaves are unfurling
Springing into life
A purpose to fulfil for the mighty tree
It's lifeline - it's lifeblood
A refuge for so many.
Fresh bright sunshine shoots down
From sapphire like skies
Skies full of clouds floating like meringues
On an island of deep blue skies.

Spring - the start of new life
When those who've been tucked away
Venture out of their winter homes
Back into the ever changing world.
A world that houses beauty but sadness
Evil and good
Life and death.

Spring - as we look towards
The hands of time springing back
- back into the depths of winter.
Spring feels like a lifetime away.
A lifetime…

So much can happen in a lifetime.
So much to embrace through these darker days.
Autumn leaves laying crisp upon the ground
Displaying an array of stunning colours
Browns, oranges, rust, apricot, fire and spice.

Perpetual cycles that Mother Nature serves up.
As sure as night follows day
Seasons march on.
Each season beholding it's own unique beauty.
If you can't see the beauty
Stop
Look
Listen
We are surrounded by it but are so often blind to it.

Life in all its glory should never be underestimated.
A thin thread separates life and death.
So whilst we live we must appreciate
Mother Nature and all she offers.
There is no greater gift than life
Spend your time wisely
Stop and smell the roses once in a while.
We are just a small part of a bigger picture.

Autumn's Leafy Gifts To Mother Nature

The leaves are slowly changing
They've gone through their cycle of life
Once fresh, green and vibrant
They are now crisp, shrivelled and dry.

The winds that they could once withstand
Now dislodge them from their branch.
As autumn moves in their lifeblood slips away.
More fragile day by day.

Until that wind, like breath on a cheek
Blows and they gently fall to the ground.
A zigzag route from top to bottom
Settling on the damp, wet ground beneath them.

Suddenly surrounding the strong trunk,
Which once supported them.
The ground now a fabulous array of autumnal colours.
Reds, browns, amber and oranges.

We dive through them, pushing them up with our feet.
A delightful crunching sound meets our ears.
We laugh as the leaves momentarily lift into the air
Before slowly settling on the ground again.

Is this the end of their purpose?
No, not at all.
Those leaves may now lie dormant on the ground
But as they slowly shrivel away their work begins.

A new role - a new purpose
To feed the ground beneath it.
For they are autumn's gift to Mother Nature
A nutrient, a lifeblood - nature's rich food.

So after their green vibrant days
They live on in another form.
I'd like to think our lives are similar.
We may not always be green and vibrant.

But every day you touch somebody's life
Making memories, creating family traditions.
Sharing kindness, laughter, love and fun.
Life is more than just the days we are "living".

I think we all live on in some way...
By the deeds we have done and the people's lives we've touched.
Never think your life isn't important- we all have something to give - no matter how small it may feel.
The smallest gesture can be the biggest moment in someone else's life.
Be the leaf that keeps on giving to your fellow trees!

Nature's Winter Wonderland

The trees are all bare - no more leaves left to show.
It's so cold my poor cheeks have a red healthy glow.
The fields have a sparkle as they are dusted with white.
The crisp white frost glistening in the morning sunlight.

The dog excitedly trots along the crisp, icy grass verge.
His paws make the grass crunch and they become submerged.
He doesn't seem to feel the cold one little bit
Well he's got a fur coat - that must be it!

He buries his nose deep into the grass.
The blades gently bend and make a snap like glass.
With the trees laid bare you can see all the birds.
They sit way up high - their song is their words.

Their chirping seems louder in the cool crisp air.
They will soon be looking for their spring love affair!
I pull my coat tighter and snuggle into my woolly, soft scarf.
I've frightened the birds they're wondering why I'm on their turf.

Crisp winter mornings actually feel quite cool.
Nature's frost making the land look like jewels.
The nights pull out slowly and the sun shines a bit more.
Meaning we can all slowly venture once again outdoors.

I can't feel my fingers, my toes or my nose!
A part of me would like to still be under my bedclothes.
I stand, take a breath and look all around.
The birds and Benji are the only sounds.

Mother Nature is awesome as she regenerates.
So many things lying deep in a dormant state.
But spring is approaching and soon the leaves will appear.
So many different cycles across the full year.

The leaves will grow and the flowers will bloom.
The daffodils, the primroses and snowdrops will boom.
They will soon be appearing in full Technicolor.
The world suddenly looks a little fuller.

So we may be in winter and it feels a bit dull.
With nothing to do but our sorrows to mull.
So pull on your big warm winter coat, scarf and gloves.
Because with the winter season there is still a lot to love.

The Great British Weather

Brrrr it's so cold I can't feel my feet!
It's like Dancing On Ice out on the street.
We've not had it this cold for so many months.
Well I think we may have had frost, just the once.

It's arctic you know, I can't feel my nose.
My whole body is frozen right down to my toes.
The weatherman said it was going to be cold.
Apparently the wind will increase sevenfold!

But didn't you hear there's rain on the way.
It's supposed to arrive tomorrow, during the day.
Oh I don't like the rain, it will be wet and windy.
As the rain droplets run off my nose I feel wimpy.

I mean it's just not like Christmas when it's warm and wet.
Did you place your annual white Christmas bet?
Be nice to see the beautiful sunshine again.
Wind and rain, tut tut, it really is such a pain.

Did you hear about poor Rita? She slipped on the ice!
In some ways having it a bit warmer would be nice.
But it just doesn't feel festive when it's damp and wet.
Thank goodness I didn't place that white Christmas Day bet.

Food For Festive Thought

A child's face is innocent and pure
Looking up at the Christmas tree in awe.
It's a whole world of beauty, sparkle and glitter
Their mouths wide open as their eyes flutter.

The lights are so bright and glow so divine
A memory that's precious - a snapshot in time.
The child just sees beauty and dancing lights
The tree brings joy brightening the dark nights.

All that child wants is to feel safe and secure
They don't want a world that's scary and unsure.
So when God sent down to earth his only son
He knew that there was much work to be done.

He advocates a world full of kindness and love
But evil and ill doing is not so easy to get rid of.
So maybe we adults should sit and reflect
How can we create a world based on respect?

The child who looks at the Christmas tree
Maybe they help hold the future's key.
They make no judgement on whether the tree is too crass
They don't slot people into some sort of class.

They just look at the world through their innocent eyes
They enjoy every moment, well maybe not the mince pies!
The tree can be big, small, simple or elaborate
The child still looks on and sees the value in it.

So this Christmas enjoy every moment
Sit back and look for atonement
Don't judge others whose journey is unknown
And let's not forget all those who are alone.

A Truly Special Day

I'm carrying a precious load
We've travelled many miles.
Despite our dusty journey
I still see Joseph smile.

I know there's something special
About to happen soon.
So I must keep plodding on
Guided by the stars and moon.

My hooves and limbs are aching
But I wouldn't stop and rest.
I know to have this honour
I have been truly blessed.

I see Joseph look at Mary
His eyes full of hope and love.
He wonders if theirs will be
A story that others may write of.

Mary smiles and thanks him
For being by her side.
Joseph promised her that
They will soon be by a fireside.

They have no wealth or riches
But they ensure I am looked after.
And despite the weary journey
I can hear their gentle laughter.

I tread as gently as I can
Because I know Mary is with child
I try my best to take it steady
And be gentle, soft and kind.

We reach our destination
But alas there is no room.
It seems our search for shelter
Sadly must resume.

I can see in Joseph's eyes
The fear that he is feeling.
An innkeeper offers them shelter
But it's really not appealing.

Joseph smiles and thanks him
As he shows them to the stable.
The floor is laced with straw
And there's a manger for a cradle.

I stand very quiet and still
As Joseph lifts Mary down.
I sense that this unborn baby
Will be a King without a crown.

The stable is cold and draughty
But Mary doesn't seem to mind.
Her son is born that night
A birth that will change all mankind.

I know my part in the story
Was just a small one to play.
But I knew the load I carried
Would change the world one day.

I look on in awe and wonder
As the baby lies asleep.
This special, precious moment
Forever in my heart I will keep.

I may be just a lowly donkey
But I had my part to play.
My instincts had told me
This would be a truly special day.

The Best Things In Life Are Free

The lights are twinkling alive and bright
It truly is a beautiful, dazzling sight.
Christmas Trees laden with decorations and memories.
Chocolates, tinsel & baubles just some of its accessories.
A wreath hangs neatly on the front door.
As we are fast approaching the end of the year.
A year that was full of highs and also some lows.
We've all lost loved ones or those we held close.

It's a time to celebrate our Saviours birth
The time that he came down to this lowly earth.
It is a time to reflect on the year gone by.
Give thanks for the good things as we bid the old year goodbye.
So while presents are piled under the tree
Let's not lose sight of reality.
The best things in life are always free.
So love, live and laugh with your family.

Spring Has Sprung…

Chitter chatter oh what a clatter, rising up from the bustling hedgerows.
It is the sound of the springtime natter, as lots of birds have made their new homes.

Homes created to welcome new life, life in a world with so much uncertainty.
Life that is balanced on the edge of a knife, life that will mean we will have birds for an eternity.

Just stop for a moment and let it all soak in; those beautiful noises as they sing out their song.
Some sound so delicate and others make a din, they will call out their birdsong all day long.

Each song is different and has its own beauty, sounds blending naturally into the background.
Each bird is busily carrying out their duty, days spent between the nest, sky and ground.

Searching out food to feed to their chicks, protecting their nests from all sorts of dangers.
They find safety in bushes, trees, shoes, even bricks! Hiding away from all sorts of strangers.

Behind every bush there is a story to tell, a poor little creature trying to perpetuate life.
Sometimes their song is a warning bell, looking out for each other to help avoid strife.

So just take that moment to stop, look and listen, you will find that there's birdsong nearly everywhere.
Think of those birds living daily with frisson, but most of all let's appreciate that spring is in the air.

Covid-19

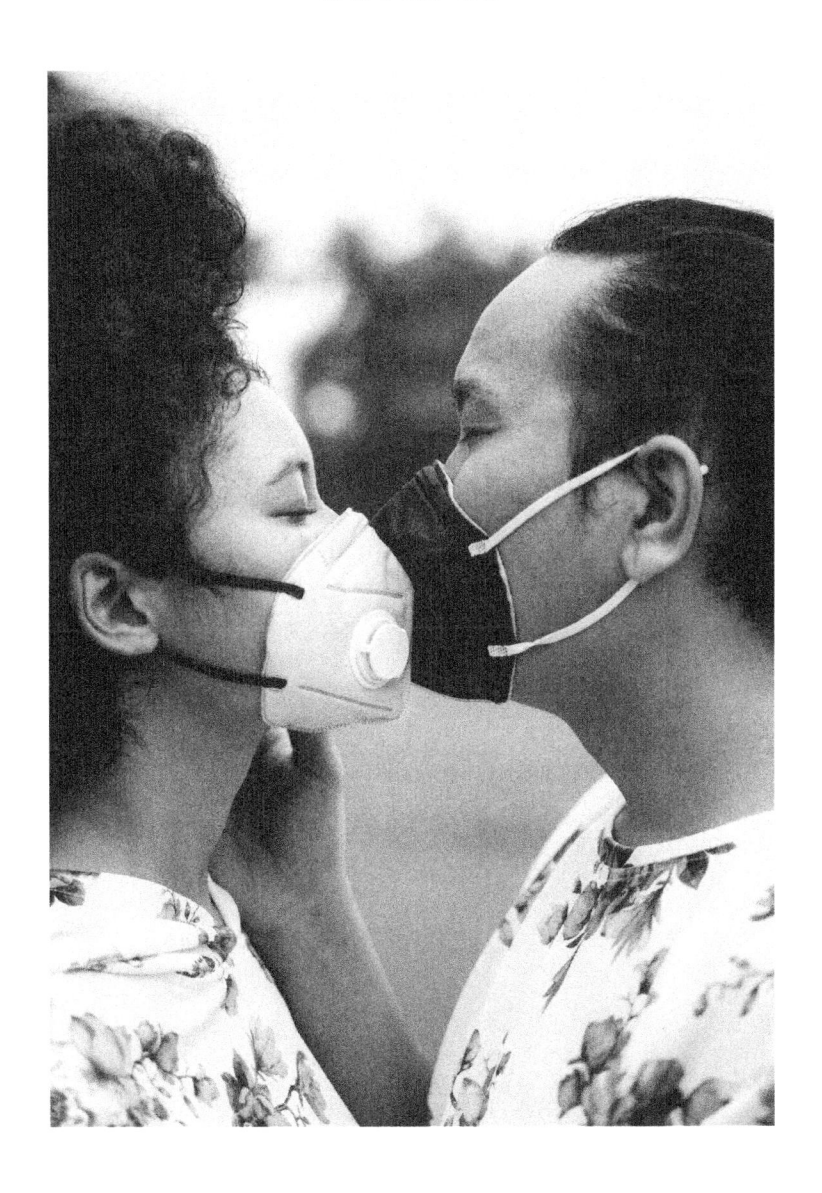

In The Stillness We Will Find Hope

In the stillness we will find hope
In the peace we will find faith
In the stillness we will find hope
We are living through this sad wraith

In the stillness we will find hope
On the dark days my heart just broke
In the stillness we will find hope
This virus slips around us like a cloak

In the stillness we will find hope
In the quiet we see so much despair
In the stillness we will find hope
This vile virus that came from nowhere

In the stillness we will find hope
Human kindness - we're wrapped in love
In the stillness we will find hope
Knowing God looks down from above

In the stillness we will find hope
In the silence we sit and pray
In the stillness we will find hope
In that moment we long for better days

Don't lose that sense of hope
Dreams vivid like a kaleidoscope
Don't lose that sense of hope
Together we will cope.

The Year That Changed The World

A simple walk has become so precious
Soaking in the views that look so luscious.
Restricted to just one jaunt a day
We must try and escape come what may.

Sadly not all can venture out
Cabin fever setting in no doubt.
The situation forced upon us
We must accept without a fuss.

But when we do step outside our door
It suddenly feels far from a chore.
Look up to the glorious skies
Whether it's sunset or sunrise.

The beauty that was there before
Think of it like your personal dance floor.
Embrace it all and soak it up
As if you are a tiny pup.

Look out with eyes afresh
See your countryside at its best
Think of those who are housebound
Who'd love to have a crowd around?

For they see no-one day to day
It's for these people we must pray
And those that are not feeling well
Who would really love to just be held.

Pubs stand empty like lifeless souls
These were once our favourite watering holes.
It used to be where we'd sup some beer
Once a place full of laughter, love and cheer.

The chapel stands majestic in the evening sun
How many times I've gone past it on my run.
It should be full of song and praise
Not just on a Sunday but all the days.

The chapel doors may be firmly locked
But God is never off the clock
And so many in their hour of need
Praying that God may intercede.

It is a time so full of worry
Previously we were all in such a hurry
We'd lost sight of the precious things
Like children playing on the swings.

So fill your lungs with that fresh air
Don't worry about your nails and hair.
Devour a much simpler life
Fill it with love - make it rife.

So please just look out for one another
Your mum, dad, children, sister and brother
Don't forget those that may be in need
And let's lose all the social greed

We will find the end of that rainbow
And finally return to the status quo
But let's not return to who we were
When 2020 is a distant blur.

You Say Hello...

You say hello and I say – oh wait don't go
It's days since I have seen another living soul!
To go out for a stroll and see no signs of life
Is a sight I would have welcomed in my normal working life.

It is like I need to ring a bell and shout out I'm unclean
As this virus really does go completely unseen.
That doesn't mean we cannot pass a moment in the street
We can smile at passing strangers, say hello to those we meet.

Lets stop and have a socially distanced chat
There can't be any harm in that.
But to be honest what news is there for us to share
Have you seen the latest Facebook post about the teddy bears?

I cannot even be bothered to do my face and hair
Although did you see that post that I took the time to share?
Angelina has a campaign she has laid out her grand plan
To dress up on Saturday nights - we will all look really glam.

I've spent a lot of time practicing my wave
I hope to use it frequently when I come out of my cave.
It is really rather regal and I feel just like a queen
So if you see my arms flailing you know you have been seen.

All my races have been cancelled but I gave a secret cheer
I cannot find my trainers let alone my running gear.
I am working on something that is really not so great
It is an increasing muffin top due to everything I ate!

I developed new habits with this enforced house arrest
They really are not ones to keep my body at its best.
I sit at my laptop with my new friend at my side
It is the faithful biscuit barrel and down my belly they do glide.

It seems that the dogs are the real winners in this deal
I cannot even use the toilet without them at my heels!
They love having humans in their every day domain
Our daily little outing around the country lanes.

So when I leave the house for my daily exercise
I know that seeing people will be the real big high.
We will stand across the road and give a nod and wave
Secretly glad we distanced - phew that was a close shave!

So get behind the campaigns that are floating round about
Like giving our NHS heroes a massive big shout out.
A rainbow in your window may help brighten someone's day
A teddy in your window is a bear hunt game our kids can play
At the end of this ordeal we will come out so much stronger
Lets hope we stand and chat for just that little bit longer.

A Faceless Future?

We none of us can know what lies ahead for us
Once the pandemic of 2020 finally settles in the dust.
There will have been great hardship and sadness all around
Tears flowing so freely but the sadness can't de drowned.

Our once hectic lives suddenly changed so much
No longer can we shake hands, fearful of that touch.
We can't enjoy a warm embrace and a hug to say hello
A close and precious gesture that we have to forego.

But I wonder what the future holds once this comes to pass
We are hoping that our children can just return to their school class.
I'm fearful for what our new strange world may look like
We will step out of the door hoping the virus doesn't strike.

But what sight will greet us as we venture through our doors
Not a sight of beaming faces as we tentatively explore.
A sea of faceless people as we all hide behind our mask
And as the sun beats upon us we cannot stop and bask.

A mask that keeps us safe but strips our emotional signs away
Covering how you're feeling, no matter what you say.
Shielding our beautiful faces, their radiance's confined
That simple piece of material supposed to give us piece of mind.

I cannot bear the thought of seeing streets of faceless people
The face that tells us how you feel, happy, sad or gleeful.
Imagine not seeing a simple wholesome smile
I do not want to see this new sort of lifestyle.

Our faces give so much to others, especially those we meet
A simple gesture of a smile as one another we do greet.
The thought of hiding our best asset underneath a mask
Covering hands and mouths becoming part of our daily tasks.

So I wonder what life will look like twelve months on from now
What rules will be in place so normal life can be allowed.
A period of separation seems a price we have to pay
But I hope I can still see your beautiful faces come what may.

Behind The Mask

What lies behind that mask you wear?
Feelings, emotions you now cannot share.
Take a moment and just think it through
Half your face covered, it can be misconstrued.

When you're screaming inside and full despair
Maybe feeling like nobody really cares.
All that is seen is your pool like eyes, not that beautiful smile
We can't read the signs that you are feeling quite hostile.

Those eyes that we see like the sea of humanity
A variety of masks displaying our vanity.
Our beautiful smiles smothered and covered
Our true emotions lying deep and undiscovered.

The eyes are the windows to the soul
Or this is what we have been told.
Can your eyes truly display your happiness and joy?
Full communication potentially may now be destroyed.

That lady who sits alone on the bus with feelings of sadness
And she has no one to talk to and no one to trust.
The couple who cannot quite believe all the madness.
The person who simply is just full of badness.

The old man whose heart simply hurts with such pain.
The joy for the girl who's been sipping champagne.
All to be read through those "windows" from now
We need to look deeper to see what's not clear.

For behind that mask lies a world we cannot see
A society which no longer feels open and free.
Consider these facts when you slide on that mask
But don't ever think it's a disagreeable task.

I know it can feel like the mask sucks away all fresh air
But we must protect one another and our wonderful healthcare.
If you think it's bad to cover your face for a moment here and there
Think of those workers who don it daily, like those giving care.

A new phase of fighting this terrible virus
Fears and emotions feeling quite heightened.
More beautiful lives potentially at risk
Covid-19's movements once again feeling brisk.

So look after each other and ask how are you?
And listen to what the other construes
For you can't see their face that shows so many signs
And remember to make sure your eyes truly shine!

Lord You Were With Us

The world has been hurting the past couple of years.
So many people endured pain and loss, shedding many tears.
A pandemic that came in and stripped bare so many lives.
A virus seeping through society where so many didn't survive
All the places of worship had to close their doors.
As people were forced to meet only outdoors.
No singing, no sermons, no prayers - not a sound.
So many people became completely housebound.
But you Lord were with us every step of the way.

Our lives changed so much in the flash of an eye.
Loved ones passed away with no chance of goodbyes.
Comforted only by a stranger holding their hand
Knowing they are passing into God's own land.
Life still went on with new lives still emerging
New mums on their own with dads left home hurting.
Heroes and heroines emerged as they carried on with their job
Many returned home tired - and all they could do was sob
But Lord, you were with us every step of the way.

Then there was a light at the end of this long painful road.
A vaccine, which gave hope as the NHS reached overload.
The scientists had developed our life saving vaccine.
A jab, which could stop this vile virus Covid-19
So finally and slowly normal life has returned.
Two years and there are so many lessons we have learned.
We must live for today and soak up the small things
For we never know what tomorrow may bring.
But you Lord are with us every step of the way.

It's easy to believe that there can be no God.
As it seems our world is fundamentally flawed.
Our hearts are breaking as we watch poor Ukrainians suffer
Families losing children, mothers, fathers, sisters and brothers.
This casts huge doubt over our faith and belief.
Our minds become bogged down with torment and grief.
But we must hold our course and put our trust in you Lord.
Faith - what is it? It is like our invisible cord.
And you Lord are with us every step of the way.

The past two years have realigned people's values.
A life full of love and laughter is what we must choose.
You can't put a value on precious memories and time.
For only the Lord knows the length of our lifetime.
So stop and take stock of what is around you.
Stop a moment longer to soak up that view.
And stand in awe and wonder at what the Lord has created.
For it's there in all its amazing glory to be fully appreciated.
And remember- the Lord is with you every step of the way.

Lunch Anyone?

Well here we are, day 53 of lockdown and it's that time of day again
What would you like for lunch I yell and the answers still the same.
Oh I don't mind anything - whatever - what have you got?
I reply with what I know will be a pointless list.

You see my husband is a fussy old sod who claims he's really not
But when it comes to lunchtime he always asks - what you got?
So here we go I think, the same charade we repeat it daily
I will now list everything and this is what he will say

No I don't like soup, you know I don't, unless you have some Oxtail
Did I have Oxtail yesterday - no I didn't - I smile but then exhale.
How about cheese on toast all bubbling, golden and hot
I'll even treat you by putting a bit of tomato on the top.

No I had that earlier in the week I don't fancy it today
I sigh and can't help but think he's playing food fore play!
How about some beans on toast they never fail to please
I see his nose start to turn up and I know he's playing lunch tease.

Right OK, it's fine I say, still smiling through my gritted teeth
Honestly my face says I love you dearly but I'm seething underneath
A nice poached egg on crisp white toast - hah that will hit the mark
Oh god he's going to reject it and that was my trump card.

How about a nice ham sandwich with all the salad trimmings
I've gone off ham to be honest - by now I'm considering slimming.
My final offer to him - a sumptuous toastie - hot and tasty
There is a glimmer of hope, he's rubbing his chin - mmm maybe.

Yes we are in - this is progress, an opening has appeared
Now I need to seal the deal before this option disappears.
A toasted sandwich with ham and cheese does that sound OK?
Mmmmm yes OK that sounds alright - oh good of you to say.

Isn't that like cheese on toast but just the other way round?
And I'm sure not two minutes earlier you said I don't like ham.
But I won't raise these points as I finally have his choice
He's finally made his mind up - hallelujah let's rejoice!

I've wasted half my lunch break leant against the door
Losing my grip on patience - eyes fixed firmly on the floor.
Maybe I should issue menu cards at the start of each day
Then we wouldn't be in this loop that each day we replay!

So lunch is sorted once again and I breathe a sigh of relief
Maybe in future I could consider sipping an aperitif.
He could study food choices for as long as he desired
While I just stand there sipping booze and slowly getting wired!

Distant Memories…

It seems a distant memory when we could walk freely down the street
A very distant memory when we could stop, shake hands and speak.
I can't remember what it feels like to receive a warm embrace
To stand and hug a loved one and put my hands upon their face.

I feel this pain inside my chest when I think of all we are missing
Like a squeeze of the hand, a long slow hug or even simple kissing.
My chest is filled with pain and hurt when I see no end in sight
I'm praying that the scientists can help us out of this plight.

I can't believe how much we took simple things in life for granted
Going to watch the rugby with all those loyal fans who chanted
A simple walk around a supermarket, idling the time away
Stopping for a chat to whomever we may meet along the way.

Long walks on the beach, listening to the waves crash upon the shore
And now we find we can hardly stray very far from our own front door.
A stroll through the woods when bluebells are in full bloom
Stopping, looking, listening and admiring a beautiful bird's plume.

It breaks my heart to not see my friends and sit and share some wine
It's feels an eternity since we all sat and laughed or went out to dine.
I'd love to go to a gig and just dance like no one is watching
My poor long suffering friends hide in shame as my dancing is so shocking!

It feels an eternity since I sat inside a theatre engrossed in a show
And now our poor theatres are struggling - will they survive - who knows?
Robbed of all our freedom our lives have been stripped bare
We are mere mortal humans with an inner need to share.

It fills me with great sadness that I cannot see my family
Months of separation sadly now a very real reality.
Those special times together are precious memories
I sit and ponder better times, a wonderful reverie.

I sit and contemplate what on earth will be our new normal
With masks, gloves and social distancing it may feel quite formal.
I yearn for our past freedoms and all we used to share
But for now we will just carry on - alert and aware.

I Long To…

I can't wait to feel the sun beating down upon my face
But not in my back garden but a very special place.
To roam beyond my village is a yearning that is growing
To run across a beach but to feel my pace slowing
I would stop and look around me - absorbing every aspect
Just stand there quietly and take a moment to reflect
To go to gorgeous Tenby and step onto silky sands
Feet sinking into golden grains and run them through my hands.

Take a run out to Stackpole and stand upon the cliffs
To soak up a beautiful view now feels like a gift.
To stroll along the coast path, the wind whistling through my hair
That's my hair that is quite skunk like and I really do despair
A white streak down my parting after weeks of isolation
I'm sure this is a ladies problem right across the nation!
I long to sit and linger over a simple cup of coffee
Served with a soft light sponge smothered with soft toffee.

My friends sat all around me as we sit and while away the time
It feels like an eternity since I've seen them - even a lifetime.
I long to visit Cumbria and admire the stunning lakes
Sit with my sister and share a massive cake!
To stroll through a sunny Saundersfoot not a care in the world
To see the boats bobbing in the harbour, yachts with sails
    unfurled.
To walk around Pembroke and look up at that great stronghold
That strong and sturdy castle that stands there oh so bold.

I want to take a long run and dive headlong into the icy sea
Not do my normal dancing act and only get in up to my knees!
So many beautiful places my heart just longs to see
A muddy stroll through a forest where Benji can climb a tree.
I've always loved our country and all it has to offer
It's now that I really appreciate all it has proffered.

Covid-19 Silver Lining…

Your normal daily life spews out CO_2
Will this lockdown change your environmental view?
We are seeing that our planet is very slowly healing
Surely the idea of cleaner air is appealing?
I know that when this is over we will all revert to type
Maybe I'm being harsh, applying wild stereotypes.
Our planet, wildlife & nature slowly being choked
We created mass industries, which produce a mass of smoke.
Our discarded waste and plastic killing ocean life
Surely we should expect better for God's wildlife.
Our fast, material lives are killing these lush lands
I hang my head in shame and hold it in my hands.
A disposable society the western world created
The consequences of our actions being unappreciated.
This terrible virus seeping across the world
It's devastating effects slowly being unfurled.
But the silver lining of this time is the opportunity to heal
This time has shown what matters and what we really feel.
So let's sit and ponder life as it was once and what could be
And dream of swimming in a clear and waste free sea.

Natures Playground

Take a moment in your day to stop and look outside your window
You will see lots of bees and birds maybe even goats but not a pink flamingo!
What a wondrous sight that would be
Pink flamingos for all to see!

Take a moment - look around - for you will hardly hear a sound.
Stand outside - arms wide - eyes to the skies and slowly turnaround.
There is a certain stillness in the air
In that moment you have no cares.

The quietness that surrounds us has become nature's playground, lockdown opened a gateway.
The creatures of God's wondrous world becoming braver day by day as human activities ebb away.
Sit a while and you will see
Birds bobbing in and out of trees.

The sun has also played its part and will burst through those dark rain clouds.
But please be careful and pay heed don't be gathering in large crowds.
Instead soak up that glorious heat
Watch birds wings never missing a beat.

What about those nuisance friends and I don't mean those upon two legs.
Think of those things you run away from like mice, spiders and daddy longlegs!
Those pesky buzzing wasps and flies
No humans swotting them as they pass by.

Natures slowly reclaiming the world, the environment sighing in relief
No more car fumes billowing into the skies causing underlying grief
We've wrapped the world in a plaster
Despite this being a global disaster

So every cloud has a silver lining and while we humans sit and suffer
Nature can truly come alive and we will all come out a little bit tougher
So take this chance to watch the show
It's natures payback don't you know.

Hands Face Space...

2020 the year of new sayings and ways
Every day waiting to hear a new phrase.
Stay at home and stay safe was the one that we heard first.
When we used to think bubbles were just things that could burst.

Along came that thing we all love to say
It's the new normal - we hear it repeated every day.
I don't want the new normal I'm screaming inside
I just want the old ways - before thousands had died.

Next they decided we must stay alert
Great another new buzz word for Boris to blurt.
I'm alert all the time; we've been living in fear.
In case someone with the virus is standing near!

Wear a mask - wash your hands - Stay 2 metres apart
We've heard most of these things right from the start.
So many renditions of happy birthday have been sung.
Ironically singing is banned and mustn't trip off our tongues!

Go out - but stay in - don't mix in large crowds.
But going to the pub is definitely allowed.
Just socially distance and all will be well
But you turn, speak and the droplets just fell...

Droplets - tiny droplets that just become airborne
Slowly and quietly invading our lungs.
Stay alert - stay apart - is that one metre or two?
All the countries having such varying rules.

Hands -face - space is the new one today.
Boris has spoken so we must all obey.
But we don't need these tag lines to know what to do
We just need common sense to protect me and you!

So remember the rules - if you know what they are
All in all it's probably best not to travel to far.
Just remember to keep your hands clean and stand far apart
After all we don't want to appear on a government bar chart!

Home Schooling - Oh What Fun!

We are going to have to isolate for a little while
But honestly we can do lots that will make us smile.
Little Lucy can draw rainbows to her hearts content
Ben can construct a Lego bridge - time that's so well spent.

We will set up a fabulous home schooling spot
I'm a little worried that I may look a like a clot.
It's going to be wonderful mummy teaching math
There won't be tears, tantrums or you seeing my wrath

We will sit for hours reading books and cuddling on the settee
We will sit a while in peace and quiet, watching buzzing bees.
It's going to be idyllic, such a precious time
Sliding out of spring into gorgeous summertime.

Two weeks on and here we are, still stuck in the house
The home school area in a pile - the chalk turned to dust.
I haven't washed my hair in days it's looking rather lank
I had to have a shower as the kids told me that I stank.

I've switched from buying bottles of wine it's better from the box
I don't know how many tines I've tripped over Ben's building
   blocks!
Lucy doesn't want to draw a picture for the key workers
Doesn't she know I need her to be quiet coz I'm now a
   homeworker.

I'm trying to stay calm - keep calm and carry on
My windows full of pictures that the kids have drawn
I will never get those marks off that dull and smeared glass
Oh jeepers now they want a picnic sitting on the grass.

No I haven't got sausage rolls, strawberries, crisps or cake
I know these are the picnic things we normally like to take.
Please don't cry again because you cannot have your way
I am fed up of explaining we must stay in, come what may.

You'd like to do some baking, the umpteenth time you've asked
Yes I know that would be great fun and it's always such a blast
But I have no butter, eggs or flour
Oh no here you go another great big howler.

My husband is so helpful sitting watching the T.V.
Moaning when we say we are going to do Oti
But you've already done Joe Wicks - P.E. in your home
His whining voice is really grating to my bones.

It's such a long day I remind him with a big wide smile
If we wear out Ben and Lucy it really will have been worthwhile.
He lets out a long big sigh handing over the remote
Why don't you take a walk I say - let me get you your coat.

Who knew there would be pressure to keep the house so clean?
Because everyone is face timing from work to Aunty Jean.
People's houses look immaculate - show houses, quite pristine
I'm just looking for a corner that sort of looks quite clean.

Oh man this isn't what I imagined; it's not the family dream
My husband and my kids are a load of drama queens.
They've fought over the iPad and what to have for lunch
I'm worrying about the future as we head for a credit crunch.

We are now living in our PJs and nobody really cares
What's the point in doing makeup, nails or hair?
The highlight of our week is the weekly national clap
To thank all the heroes - a chorus all gift-wrapped.

I'm so glad it is Easter and the schoolwork put to bed
I don't know how these teachers really don't go off their heads.
Who knew teaching could be so fraught with much frustration
That glass of deep rich red wine has been my one salvation!

Don't be fooled by those social media posts where families look
 idyllic
They will drive you round the bend and make you imbecilic.
That photo is a snap shot not showing what went before
When the kids were lying face down crying on the floor.

So don't be too hard on you, them or him
Even when times are feeling pretty grim.
It's just a chapter in our lives
The true key is to survive.

Rainbow Nails…

I've got teddy bears in my window and time upon my hands
I've stocked up on my loo roll & I've a cupboard full of cans.
I need to paint a rainbow for the entire world to see
And I find myself obsessing because I saw a big fat bee.
I'm standing on my drive clapping with my friends
Then rushing back inside as my hands I need to cleanse.
I've learnt I've been washing my poor hands oh so wrong
Apparently we need to do it to a good old sing a long
My post is being delivered by a newfound superhero
And the miles I've put upon my car are a big fat zero!
I never thought I'd stand and wash my shopping clean
My shopkeeper serving me from behind a massive screen!
My home is now my sanctuary, a place to keep us safe
People donning gloves and masks upon their face.
Our wonderful world has been turned upon its head
But now we're looking out for each other instead.
So paint your nails in rainbow colours
And put your hair into those rollers.
We need to look our best as we clamber through this crisis
And remember that to live is a prize that is just priceless.

NHS Heroes

Never faltering, giving up or giving in
Heroes is too small a word for the part they play
Singing in virtual choirs for you, for me and for Captain Tom

Helping in every way they know
Eagerly waiting for the day they can hug their family and friends again
Remembering all those that have lost the battle
Optimistic that the UK and world will win this invisible war
Exhausted and tired, waiting for the day they can truly relax and unwind
Smiling, laughing and full of hope for the future

Because they've got this and we trust them - they are doing the best they can for our beautiful UK.

The Real Heroes 2020

You slip out of house at the start of your day
Ready to face what may come your way.
You don't wear a cape or boast of your deeds
Helping so many who are in such need.

You go about your day and never complain
You don't ever let your patients see your pain.
Your focus is them and helping them through this
All your feelings of sadness you have to dismiss.

You have to stay strong to fight the invisible monster
Some days you feel you can't go on too much longer.
The public are there for you cheering you on
But the sadness of loss is sometimes too strong.

You often feel broken and unable to cope
But to all that you meet you radiate hope.
Your hearts are in pieces for the ones that we lost
Because you want to save lives at any cost.

We are clapping for carers and all our key workers
Most of the UK feel like some strange observers.
Staying at home to protect precious lives
Wishing Covid-19 into the archives.

Through the darkest days there are glimmers of hope
Captain Tom raising millions to help the NHS cope.
Sometimes you just sit exhausted and weep
Wishing your tired body could just get some sleep.

You truly are heroes without superpowers
Working daily into the wee small hours
You gently hold their hand as they slip away
You sit there with them, maybe even pray.

You know that their loved ones can't be at their side
Those last precious moments their family denied
So you sit and you give them the comfort they need
Inside it makes your poor broken heart bleed.

But you know that there are many who beat this disease
The joy on their face as the ward they can leave
Beating this virus feels like a throw of the dice
In debt to the health service for the rest of our lives.

So as sad as it seems as each day slowly passes by
We try to stay strong and we try not to cry.
Our values have changed in the blink of an eye
Filled with sadness as some have said their last goodbye.

So you see you're our heroes - you are wonderful people
We cheer in our streets and ring bells from church steeples!
The role that key workers play is so vital
Superheroes is definitely your new job title.

There are not enough words to show our gratitude
For deliveries, cleaning, policing and our food.
So many brave people go out every day
Risking their lives - so it's for them that we pray.

So if you know someone who's going to work
Leaving their loved ones as regular as clockwork.
Stop for a moment and give thanks for their part
Make sure your thankfulness comes from your heart.

Summer Vibes - Coz There's No Christmas Tribes!

I'm thinking of having an alternative Christmas
Creating a beach scene - cocktails not biscuits
Now hear me out for you must think me mad
Not to go festive, surely that can only be bad?

The tree will be up and the lights gently flickering.
The house full of treats and the garden is glimmering.
A fully lit 6-foot Santa stands in pride of place
Stockings hanging up in the candlelit fireplace.

It sounds quite idyllic - it truly does
Because Christmas always brings an amazing buzz.
But what about parties and pre-Christmas drinkies
No shaking of hands not even our pinkies!

Surrounded by things that just scream out family
No drunken renditions of Queen's Bohemian Rhapsody!
No parties or swift after work gin and tonics
Moaning that your spending has been really chronic.

So if I sit in some sand with a pina colada
Maybe even pretend I'm in the Costa Brava
Then I may find no socialising a less bitter pill to swallow
Either way I promise I won't sit and wallow!

What's Your Value?

Cast your mind back to a time not that long ago.
When we were confined to our houses and had nowhere to go.
Did you notice at that time there was an interesting shift.
It wasn't the actors, singers and footballers that we missed.

It was the health service workers who helped keep us alive.
It was scientists working tirelessly for a way for us to survive.
We went outside and clapped for them, they were heroes one and all.
We were proud if we knew a doctor, nurse or carer always on call.

They risked their lives to save others, at a time we lived in fear.
We were petrified and just wanted to keep our loved ones near.
They looked like aliens behind all their gowns and masks.
They carried out their duties, a list of endless tasks.

And the footballers could do nothing but think outside the box.
As their careers were taken and smashed on the Covid-ridden rocks.
The public outcry was loud, the health service was our saviour.
Families were in turmoil and some shed many a tear.

The world suddenly turned human value completely on its head.
Crying out that these people were so much, so we should pay them more instead.
Yes we missed our arts and the creators but they couldn't save a life.
Footballers "worth millions" couldn't spare families from this strife.

How quickly we've forgotten what those people all went through.
So much heartache and despair, at the time we wished it wasn't true.
I will never comprehend how some jobs hold such high value.
Surely as society we can do things better than we do?

Our Queen

Lilibet 1926-2022

Like a carpet of bluebells you radiated beauty.

Inspirational speeches and a conduct so regal.

Loved by so many across the whole globe.

Incredible woman - married to your royal duties.

Brave and courageous even in your darkest hours.

Elegant, graceful, wise and always serene.

'Twas an honour for us to call you our Queen.

Monarch, Leader, Woman And Mother

The day has come when your long reign is over
There is a beautiful bridge for you to pass over
Where it goes nobody really knows
Your faith assured you there are no dark shadows

You were a woman standing strong for all
Who will be in all our hearts forever more
You were a true lady full of love and grace
Unique and really impossible to replace

You were a leader who many looked up to
Always knowing the right thing to do
Standing for honesty, peace and truth
The nations mood you could always soothe

The day has come for you to meet your maker
You know you've always been God's caretaker
Your faith was strong and you steered us well
You were a devout Christian as we could tell

The pain of grief that we now bear
Is great, but we take comfort in prayer
Wonderful memories your people now share
It's easy to see just how much we all care

The journey you make now is one of glory
Your life unfolded into a beautiful story
Now you will be with your precious Prince Philip
Your soul mate to whom you lovingly looked up

He was by your side through thick and thin
Once again you're united, as a new era begins
You gave us all so many fond memories
Moments that will be remembered for centuries

A monarch who reigned for over 70 years
Never once did you display your fears
You guided us with your ever-steady hand
You truly loved our beautiful land

Above all else you were a mother
You instilled the need to love one another
Your family will do you proud
Charles has taken his solemn vows

So now it's time to say goodbye
You are as free as a heavenly butterfly.
So slip your hand into your beloved Philip's
He will keep you safe, so don't you worry about us

In memory of our Queen Elizabeth II 1926-2022

Our Queen 1926-2022

We can't believe you are gone
But we know we must all carry on.
You served us with respect and love
A monarch who we were truly proud of.

A life devoted to your people
You truly were a queen for all people.
You reigned with dignity and respect
Your reign was, simply put - perfect.

You always had a twinkle in your eye
Your passing leaves such hue and cry
A woman full of grace and beauty
Married to your noble duty.

Prince Philip was always by your side
A tower of strength he did provide.
He was your soul mate and your rock
There for you around the clock.

You were never born to be our Queen
Your reign is one we are blessed to have seen.
You stood up for all that was true and right
Guiding your people with goodness and light.

You endured to be true and honest
Serving your people as you promised.
A life devoted to your public duty
Your smile was radiant, a thing of beauty.

Your passing has made my heart ache
Shedding a tear when I heard the news break.
You've always been in our lives,
The longest reign recorded in the archives.

We were blessed to call you our Queen
The like of which nobody's ever seen.
You bridged the gaps in our society
Displaying a true model for propriety.

Now you've fallen into your last sleep.
Many shedding tears and will weep.
We can't imagine a life without you
It's time for us to pay our respects to you.

We will hold you in our hearts forever
You were quite simply our national treasure.
So now we grieve with heavy hearts
However now our new King's reign starts.

So rest in peace ma'am - you will be missed.

A Corgi's Love

I'm sat patiently waiting for your return
I hear a noise, sit up and turn.
It's not you - I lay back down
I don't understand why you aren't around.

I miss our daily walk and chat
I knew you were a mastered diplomat.
But when with me you were kind and gentle
A lady who was truly non judgemental.

I'd noticed that your steps had slowed
Signs of your age had begun to show.
I didn't care how quickly we walked
You still looked lovingly at me as you talked.

Now I sit and begin to wonder
What if we've been put asunder?
A world without you by my side
The thought leaves me terrified.

I'd lay my head upon your lap
Your arms around my body you'd wrap.
I'd look up at you through my big brown eyes
I knew that you were old but oh so very wise.

And now I don't know where you are
I fear this may be our au revoir.
I sense you've gone on your next journey
I don't know why you left without me.

So now I sit here in the sunshine
Alone and lost - I begin to pine.
My lead is hanging up by the door
Walkies with your majesty are no more.

The love between a dog and its owner
Is the greatest I could ever have shown her.
Only I could keep safe her fears and thoughts
That she'd disclosed on our long walks.

So it is that I'm now left all alone
Our special relationship is unbeknown.
I was there for you day to day
I'd always listen and obey.

So as you ascend onwards to heaven
I hope your people have learnt a lesson.
To live a life that's true and honest
As for us, we'll meet again - I promise.

Your Final Journey 1926-2022

And so it is that the sun is setting on this historical day.
A day filled with thanksgiving and we saw a nation pray.
Your coffin laid onto a large heavy gun carriage.
Bound for Westminster Abbey, where you were married.

A carriage that once carried your father, the King.
The Abbey filled with glorious sounds as choristers sing.
The place of your coronation - the start of a 70 year reign.
The day that you passed away filled us with so much pain.

One hundred and forty two naval seamen undertook their duty.
A military procession filled with spectacular beauty.
So the nation and world could reflect on your life.
Today was not the day for disagreements or strife.

Your coffin is adorned with a crown, orb and sceptre.
You always knew that God was your great protector.
In the peace and the silence the tenor bell tolled 96 times.
One for each year of your life that bell did chime.

The sun streamed down and in through stained glass windows.
In the great architectural abbey lay no deep, dark shadows.
Upon your coffin lay a simple wreath of home flowers.
Each of the blooms having a reason for their assemblance.
Myrtle for marriage and Rosemary for remembrance.

The day thou gavest, Lord, is ended but your legend begins.
For you, our Queen have truly gained your Angel wings.
A young Prince and Princess wanted to be part of this day.
You were their shepherd, guiding them along their way.

A nation fell silent - simply united in gladness but also grief.
A comfort to so many was knowing that you had great faith.
Each corner of the abbey filled with singing and praise.
Your relentless hard work, dedication to duty - never ceased to amaze.

In the place where you married and were given your crown.
You vowed to all your people you'd never let them down.
Throughout your long reign you led from deep within your soul.
And now it is God's dwelling place where you now shall go.

Your faith comforted you, as death opened the door to glory.
You would have known that you were stepping into holy territory.
Nothing can separate mankind from the love of God.
Though we are sure that, sometimes, even your life was flawed.

As you left Westminster Abbey the crowds were amassed.
A ripple of applause, like waves, rose up as you passed.
The people threw flowers as a symbol of gratitude.
This sight was a wall of thanks in such magnitude.

A sea of red accompanied you down the long Mall.
A Queen who wanted so much to be seen by all.
Onwards you travelled to your great home, Windsor
Where thousands lined the streets - hoping to see Her.

Then in the depths of St George's chapel a son pays his respect.
Laying out the company camp colour - taking a moment to reflect.
Symbols of your reign now removed from your coffin.
Know this ma'am, your reign will never be forgotten.

All lives have a beginning and an end - alpha and omega.
So it is now we must look forward to a bright new era.
A lone piper stands and plays his final lament.
A monarch, our Queen, he was proud to represent.

So as the sound of the piper slowly faded away
It was a final farewell on this historic day.
Gun salutes were heard as the Sebastopol bell rung out.
For a mother, a queen, a leader and a Christian devout.

So now as our period of national mourning comes to end.
We give thanks for a long life that was truly a godsend.
It is now that your family and our King can grieve.
As momentary from public life they can take their leave.

A numbness and disbelief that you are actually gone.
A gracious, regal lady who was truly hands on.
Now your throne awaits you in heaven.
Take your rightful place as to where you ascend.

About The Author

Joanne lives near Tenby in West Wales with her husband, George and her two dogs Benji and Lucy Lou. She has two grown up children, Georgina and Dominic, who have both left home and now have families of their own. She has lived in Pembrokeshire for most of her life, moving there when she was just one year old. It is a beautiful part of the world to live in and helps to inspire Joanne with her new found love of writing.

Joanne spent most of her working life in various office roles from buyer to internal audit to school business management (with a few other things in between!). Fed up with the "rat race" she took the brave decision to resign from her full-time job and see which path life took her down. Nowadays you will find Joanne in a local coffee shop in Tenby - not sampling the coffee and cakes but serving them.

Her new part-time job gives her more time to focus on the things she loves. Like spending more time with her family, walking her dogs in the glorious Pembrokeshire countryside and beaches. Of course, she also has more time to focus on writing her blog, poetry and prose.

Joanne's new life motto - feel the fear and do it anyway!

Life is short and the one thing none of us is promised is time so spend each day wisely - it's a gift.

Published by

www.publishandprint.co.uk

Printed in Great Britain
by Amazon